Les VAMPIRES

LUCY CAVENDISH

Artwork by Jasmine Becket-Griffith

BLUE ANGEL®
PUBLISHING

LES VAMPIRES
Ancient Wisdom & Healing Messages
from the Children of the Night

This redesigned edition printed 2026
Copyright © 2014 Lucy Cavendish
Artwork Copyright © 2014 Jasmine Becket-Griffith

Published by Blue Angel Publishing®
10 Trafford Court, Wheelers Hill,
Victoria, Australia 3150
E-mail: info@blueangelonline.com
Website: www.blueangelonline.com

Edited by Tanya Graham

Blue Angel is a registered trademark of Blue Angel Gallery
Pty Ltd.

ISBN: 978-1-922574-60-2

FSC MIX Paper FSC® C007683

Printed on sustainably sourced paper,
with soy-based ink.

*I will not
let you go
into the
unknown
alone*

BRAM
STOKER

CONTENTS

LES VAMPIRES: LIFTING THE VEIL

You are about to meet the most elegant, most lonely, and most seductive Guardians of them all …

This magickal guidebook will introduce you to the powerful, ancient Les Vampires, and includes comprehensive instructions on how to safely connect with them, how to work with your cards, and three easy-to-learn spreads to give you readings of extraordinary support and clear guidance when working through a time of difficulty or loss in your life.

LET ME HAVE THE HONOUR OF INTRODUCING YOU TO THE denizens of a realm of mystery, legend and power. Within these pages, and on each of these magickal cards, you will be introduced to beings whose messages, expertise and commitment to guiding you is unsurpassed. For this world is now ready to be opened to us all, and these beings are ready to help—and be helped—by you.

Les Vampires come to those who are undergoing a test. If a shadow has fallen over your life, if you are confronting the unknown, you may feel abandoned and lonely, as if there is no light, no guide, and no path to follow.

This is the time when we have need of those who walk the hidden paths of the Dark Forest, the ones who have made the Night their home, the guardians who can help you find your way back to the Dawn.

It is time for you to receive the support of the beautiful creatures called Les Vampires.

WHO ARE LES VAMPIRES?

POWERFUL, ELEGANT AND OUTCAST, LES VAMPIRES HAVE been born, most often unwillingly, into a life which is dark and dangerous. To survive they have been urged again and again to give in to the most predatory aspects of Self. There have been many tales, many stories, and many half-told truths shared about them. Therefore, it is natural to feel wary. But like many other otherworldly creatures, somehow human, yet completely "other", these beings are often misunderstood.

For they are creatures like us – they were once human, and walked in the Light. Unlike us they will not die: they are confined to evolving within one unchanging form. They also face, with unflinching awareness, a great test – to overcome their own hunger. The beings you will meet within these pages and depicted so richly in the paintings by

Jasmine Becket-Griffith come from different places, times and cultures – but as Les Vampires, they are all complex and alluring, thrilling and powerful. They are often feared, and sometimes their isolation has led to great suffering and utter loneliness. They cannot see the light of the Sun, and must live on moonlight alone. But now, at this time, and through this deck, they can be by your side, day or night, with their wisdom, their guidance, their teachings – born of experience. For you too are on the verge of life-changing lessons.

WHY WOULD LES VAMPIRES HELP ME?

LES VAMPIRES HAVE HAD A NOBLE QUEST ASSIGNED TO them – and that is to serve Innocents. Innocents are human beings who are struggling with their own vulnerabilities, people who have been drained, in many ways, of their life force. To amend for some of their own former transgressions, The Children of the Night have received an assignment to help you – because in doing so, they will help themselves. They are abundant in all that you need at this time – rich in messages to offer, lessons to teach, and wisdoms to share with you. Be aware – Les Vampires are patient. They have all the time in the world. If they have been given a mission to care for you, and protect you, and assist you in a time of darkness, Les Vampires won't give up.

They will come to you, again and again with the express and only desire to be of assistance to you in Dark times now, and in Dark times ahead.

WHY WORK WITH LES VAMPIRES?

WE LEARN LANGUAGES BEST FROM A PERSON WHO SPEAKS the language and knows how to pronounce and shape the words. We learn a new sport best from someone who has practiced the same sport, who is familiar with all its nuances. We learn music best from those who play, and dancing from those who know the steps we wish to follow. The very best counsellors, mentors and guides in the human planes are those who have suffered the very same curses their clients bring to them to ease, heal and learn from. The school of experience is the very best there is. These Children of the Night have walked the same path you do now. They know this place, better than anyone. When it comes time to descend into the darkness it is far better to have by your side a guide who knows and understands the unfamiliar territory you have found yourself in – and one who has a clear mission, and a profound reason to help you.

HOW WILL YOU KNOW THEY ARE WITH YOU?

YOU WILL SOON BEGIN TO RECEIVE MESSAGES, IN VERY safe, secure ways from Les Vampires. They will literally light your way, helping you see what you could not see before. Masks will drop away from people and situations. You will be able to see the path that lies ahead, and you will have clear ideas, know the best action to take, and how to proceed. You will have an increased perception, be more aware of danger, or harmful influences, and know automatically who and what is worthy of your trust. Your timing and speed of reaction will greatly improve. You can begin to discern between healthy and unhealthy situations, places, people and choices – and if you have any doubt over the best course of action, Les Vampires will step in and help you see even more clearly the potential future unwinding ahead of you.

As they are so powerfully gifted, your own clairvoyance, clairsentience, clairaudience and other intuitive abilities, including telepathy, will grow stronger, and become more accurate.

Because of their love of knowledge, the perfect books, teachers, courses and information will find you, effortlessly. Because they know what it is to be so very alone, they will help you see that no matter how insignificant you once may have felt, or how lost you now find yourself; you will find a home, and you will know you are worthwhile and that you matter. Above all, you will see that you are never alone.

WHAT LES VAMPIRES WILL HELP YOU WITH

ONE OF THEIR WONDERFUL ATTRIBUTES, BECAUSE OF THEIR own struggle in overcoming their hunger, is that they can help you to overcome habits and traits that have held you back, or created illness, division and discord in your life. They also allow you to honestly undertake a kind of self-inventory, where you will forgive yourself for the seemingly harmful or selfish actions you may have taken throughout this lifetime. They will lift from you the self-hatred and the shame you have been so burdened with, and need live with no longer. They can help you release resentment and bitterness that is perpetuating harmful relationships, memories and patterns in your life. They will help you tap into your own vitality, and appreciate your simple, beautiful humanity.

They are Guardians – and one of their great talents is their ability to help you clear and free yourselves from everyday sociopaths, bullies, victims, gossips and narcissists. You will begin to recognise toxic people and toxic traits, which drink and drain your life force. There are those who have not learned, and will perhaps never learn, how to generate their own energy – you will no longer allow them into your orbit. Les Vampires will help you grow strong, and avoid these very people, and their efforts to take your energy away. The less contact you have with such people and situations, the more real and honest you become about your own vulnerabilities, and the stronger and brighter your own energy will become. This will mean you have plentiful time, renewed energy and you will be full of inspiration to devote to people and projects you really care about – including yourself. Your priorities will shift, and life will feel more balanced, secure, joyful and fulfilling.

ARE VAMPIRES REAL ?

MANY PEOPLE BELIEVE THAT VAMPIRES ARE A FICTIONAL creation. But all the brilliantly imagined fictions, from the folktales told around fires to the Vampires in popular culture phenomena like Twilight, have their origins in something true. Within all cultures, and throughout all time, there are tales of those who walk the Night. From Ancient Greece, we learn of the *vrykolakas*, vampiric beings who wore the pelt of the wolf … in Dionysian lore, we recoil at the deadly dance of the Maenads, who tore their victims to pieces with hands and teeth, so consumed by the trance and bloodlust of the worship of Dionysus.

This metamorphosis of the Vampires has seen them transform from cursed lovers of Zeus (like the Lamia you will find in this deck) to the historic truth of the 15th century Transylvanian Prince, Vlad III of the House of Draculesti, also known as Vlad the Impaler, thanks to his signature, gruesome execution style, which helped him become one of the inspirations for the fictional Count Dracula. In 19th century United States, young Mercy Brown was accused of vampirism by her own father, her corpse exhumed and violated to prevent her walking the night. As recently as the 1970s, at the atmospheric and haunting Highgate Cemetery in London, two magicians, Sean Manchester and David Farrant held a strange competition – to see which magus could find a Vampire said to be unearthing the dead at Highgate. And in July 2013, builders were shocked when they unearthed a 16th century vampire burial ground in Poland. Historians are still examining the seven skeletons, with their heads removed, and placed between their legs – a medieval practice to ensure the dead would not rise from their coffins.

A MODERN VAMPIRE STORY
MERCY BROWN

1892, RHODE ISLAND. A YOUNG WOMAN CALLED MERCY Brown used to spend nearly every day at the Chestnut Hill cemetery, visiting the resting places of members of her family who had passed as a result of an epidemic of tuberculosis. Within weeks she was taken by the disease that had already ended the lives of her mother and sister. Mercy was buried alongside them in a tomb. Soon after, her father George horrified relatives and friends by claiming that Mercy's spectre was haunting him, coming to him every night, begging for food as she was hungry. But this haunting was not exclusive. It was not long before Mercy's brother Edwin fell ill with tuberculosis – and he revealed he too had been visited by the starving spectre of Mercy, pleading for her hunger to end. The townsfolk, along with George Brown, dug up the three graves. Mercy Brown's body was not decomposed – leading George and the townsfolk to believe she was now a vampire. They removed her heart, burnt it, and mixed the ashes with water and gave this horrible potion to Edwin, still sick from tuberculosis. Mercy Brown's story became legend, and her spirit is said to walk the Chestnut Hill Graveyard to this day.

WORKING WITH *LES VAMPIRES*

BEFORE YOU BEGIN TO WORK WITH THIS DECK, PLEASE bless, or consecrate, your cards. To consecrate them is to connect, deeply, with your cards, and to make a commitment to working with them in safe and healthy ways. Because these are strong energies, it is wise to do this. (In truth, it is always wise to do this, regardless of how "light" the energies of an oracle deck may appear to be.) Remember, Les Vampires are here to help you, but just as you would treat a lion with respect, so too we must approach Les Vampires with a similar awareness.

First, be sure to clear your own sacred reading space. This process can be as simple as lighting a white candle, and placing a circle of salt around it. As the candle burns down, the energy in your space will be cleared. You will feel a shift in the energy of the space almost immediately. Smudging, or burning incense can also be helpful.

A Ceremonial Blessing of your Deck

WITH THIS DECK, I RECOMMEND LIGHTING A LITTLE incense – Les Vampires adore frankincense which also has protective qualities, and will banish any negative energies or entities. When the smoke is billowing nicely, pass your cards through once, twice, three times.

> *"Les Vampires of thee I ask*
> *To help me now with this my task."*

Say thankyou to Great Spirit, The Universe, the God and the Goddess, and then let the incense stick or resin burn down.

When you connect with this deck, you are not only connecting with external, independent energies. You are also connecting with parts of yourself which have been repressed – sometimes a large amount of energy has been exhausted with denying or rejecting these parts of yourself. You may find that there are elements of your personality, or history, or family which come up as you work with Les Vampires. You may not like some of them! But once you can bring them into the open, examine them, find a way to work with them that is healthy, and integrate these aspects into your self, you will have far more energy, and feel far less guilt, shame and confusion. You may also experience times when you seem harder, more cynical, more suspicious and skeptical than you would normally perceive yourself to be. While this can feel disturbing to people who wish to stay "bright and positive" it is worth remembering that these energies are coming forth so you can clearly evaluate what is taking place in your life at the moment. Connecting with these cards, their energies, and these aspects of yourself is a little like connecting with the raven, rather than the swan, or the dragon, rather than the unicorn. There are times when that piercing, straightforward, unflinching energy is needed. Now is that time.

How to Shuffle your Cards

THERE ARE MANY WAYS TO DO THIS. SOME PEOPLE FOLLOW the traditional two-handed shuffle, others "stir" the cards laid out before them, others fan the cards and pick them at random. Some stir with the left hand (the side most often associated with the feminine and thus the intuitive) and select with the right (the hand/side of the body most associated with the masculine, and thus the active). Find a way that works best for you. These cards can be quite large for many people—including me—thus I shuffle holding the cards length-wise. Whichever way you shuffle, it is an integral part of the process of stirring your current energy into the cards, which enhances the brew that becomes the reading, and makes messages come through clearly.

You may also like to keep a magickal journal while working with any of my decks – I particularly recommend having a journal for each deck, so that you can compare your readings. This journal is often called a Book of Shadows, or a Book of Shadows and Light, or even the old word, Grimoire is used. When you record your readings it will be very effective for learning the card meanings, and comparing results from various decks. This can also be wonderful if you are a professional reader – helping you to see patterns manifesting, seasonal variations, and the history of the seekers you are reading for.

Reading for Others

IF READING FOR ANOTHER, I FEEL IT IS ALWAYS BEST TO allow the other person—the Seeker, or Querant—to shuffle the cards, and then hand them back to you after cutting the deck and putting them back together. This way, the Seeker can truly know, in a physically real way, that they have incorporated their own energy into the reading. This eradicates the logical mind's protests and resistance, and allows you to help people more quickly and effectively. When we do our work like this, it is absolutely essential to cleanse and clear our decks frequently.

LES VAMPIRES LAYOUTS

The Trinity

TAKE LES VAMPIRES AND SHUFFLE THEM WHICHEVER WAY
is best for you, or for the person you are reading for. Hold
your question, dilemma or concern in your mind. Cut the
deck into three with your non-dominant hand (intuitive,
usually left) and put the deck back together. When you feel
this is complete, take one card from the top of the deck.

Lay this to the left.

Take the next card from the top of the deck.

Put this in the centre.

Take the final card for this layout from the top of the
deck once again.

Put this to the right.

These three cards, the Trinity, offer a complete look at
what you are facing in the situation.

The card to the left is the Underneath. It gives you clues
as to the influence of the past, and what has impacted upon
you. Les Vampires in this case are revealing something
important to you. Look at this card, and see what in the
past was of this nature, and now read the guidebook, so you

can understand it more. You are going to have to work with this spread to understand it.

The second card in the middle is The Heart. This is what is taking place at the moment and what is the central issue in the situation. It may also be the greatest challenge confronting you at this time. Again, Les Vampires are removing the veil to help you see more clearly.

The third card, The Promise, to the right represents the future manifestation of the situation given what is currently taking place and what has already happened. Look at the card, and see what will soon be confronting you – and know this can be modified or worked with, as it is dependent on what takes place from this moment forth.

With every card definition, you will see that there is a blessing and a curse. The blessing refers not just to the upright position of the card, it refers to the most positive attribute of the situation the Vampire within is showing you. If you receive it in a reversed position, the curse is going to be more influential. It is essential to know that even if you receive the card in a reversed position, and you see the word "curse", that this can be lifted through right action, and you will receive guidance as to how exactly to do this, in the section "Working with this card." Do not be fearful – this knowledge is going to save you a great deal of potential difficulty.

A Light in the Darkness

IF YOU FEEL ABANDONED, HOPELESS AND LIKE A CHILD lost in the dark at this time, and wish to know who can be of assistance with the next stage of the journey, simply pull a card and see which of Les Vampires comes forward to speak with you.

The Path through the Night

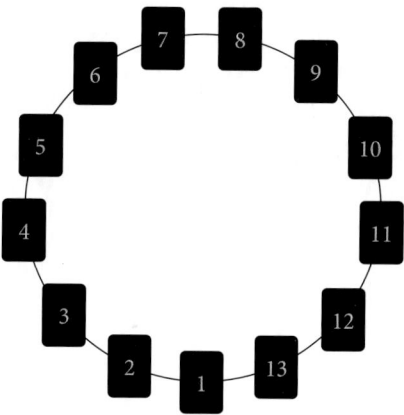

THIS IS A WONDERFUL SPREAD TO USE FOR BOTH SHORT- and long-range forecasts.

Again, contemplating your question, shuffle and cut the deck into three, moving them back into one pile with your non-dominant hand. You are going to be using the first thirteen cards from the top of the deck.

Lay these in a circle, one by one, starting at the bottom of the circle (the 6 o'clock position on a clock), moving clockwise around, until you have thirteen cards in a circle. There are several ways timing can be indicated when using this spread. If you wish to do a short-term reading, the thirteen cards can represent the next thirteen days. If you would like to do a longer term reading, you can assign a moon to each of the thirteen cards, so that the timing covers a year and a day (the thirteen moons of the solar year). Whether you choose to make this reading a thirteen day, thirteen moon, thirteen years or thirteen hours spread, the themes for each card's position remain the same.

First card: The Darkness
Second card: The Path's First Test
Third card: Obstacle and Struggles
Fourth card: The Burden to Leave Behind
Fifth card: The Teacher in the Dark
Sixth card: The Gift of the Night
Seventh card: What Will Serve You
Eighth card: What Will Test You
Ninth card: How to Recover
Tenth card: The Greatest Lesson
Eleventh card: The End Begins
Twelfth card: The Birth of the Light
Thirteenth card: A New Time

The Byzantine Cross

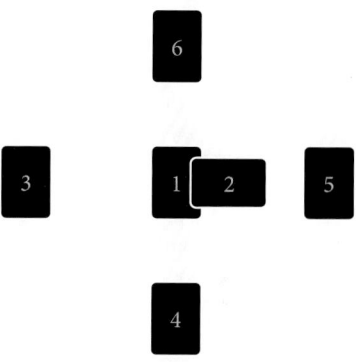

I LOVE TO WORK WITH CRYSTALS WHILE I LAY OUT THIS spread, as it adds to the opulent feel that the true Byzantine Crosses have. Studded with jewels and gold, these crosses ask us to consider that our own suffering is precious, not for the pain it has brought us, but for the lessons and insights the experience has taught us.

A basic version of this spread requires six cards. Hold your question in your mind, or speak it out loud. Shuffle your deck, then cut it into three piles with your non-dominant hand. Put these back together, as usual.

Imagine the shape of the cross. From the top of the deck, deal out your cards. In the middle, where the arms of the crucifix crossover, place a card. This represents you. Place a card over this, horizontally. This represents what is restraining, inhibiting or harming you.

Place a card to the left, where the end of the cross-arm would be. This represents the past, what has created the current circumstances.

Place a card below, at what would be the end of the pole of the cross. This represents you, now, and the influences about you.

Place a card to the right, this represents the future influences which will come to bear.

Place a card above, at the highest point of the cross. This represents the highest action you can take, the outcome, and the greatest good to strive for.

*Les Vampires have no fear of this ancient symbol, which pre-dates Christianity. They have sought answers from every spiritual system in the world, and religious symbols hold no power over them – they are simply a form, which offers opportunity for wisdom.

WITH EACH SPREAD, GIVE YOURSELF TIME TO CONTEMPLATE the images, and the words on the card. Let messages come to you quite intuitively. Please do use the guidebook and the messages within it – this is essential with this deck. You will find that each card has its own flavour and energy, depending on the being or beings who are represented by the image on the card. All are safe, and all have wisdom to teach and share.

When working with these cards it is important to remember you are very safe. You are in the hands of those who wish only to warn you, guide you, and work with you. They acknowledge their darkness, and they are honest. They are restrained. It is a little like an encounter with Aslan, the Lion King from "The Lion, the Witch and the Wardrobe", or an ancient warrior from wilder, harsher times. He is fearsome, and powerful, but he is on your side.

May your voyage into the Dark Night of the Soul enrich your life in every way. May you emerge stronger, with trust in yourself, and your perception. May you never have to pass that way again. But if ever you find the darkness reaching to take you, know that Les Vampires are here, within the energy of this deck, to help you. Unconditionally.

For the service they render to you is the source of their own salvation. The cord between you is under your control, and is woven with good intentions, and sacred actions.

Be blessed, and may the God and the Goddess watch over you.

LUCY CAVENDISH
Waxing Moon, August 2013

Card Messages

1. *Eternal Youth*

ENERGY, NEWNESS, VITALITY

LES VAMPIRES SPEAK: The quest to remain young has never been more fervent than in your time. Everywhere we—and you—look, you will observe the obsession with being, and remaining line-less. Yet there are those who are young in their face and body, who are withered with age within their souls. Youthfulness cannot be found so much in the unwrinkled face, and the muscle without atrophy. The true youth is the one who never ceases to look at the world with wonder. The truly youthful human is the one who moves, breathes and lives with delight and fervour – with a sense of discovery. Those who have accepted imprisonment, order, stasis and the inevitability of slow corruption, who no longer engage the gifts of the mind and the body, as well as those whose spirits feel tired and jaded, who endlessly complain about ageing, and who compare themselves to images created by technology, are old before they need be. For Les Vampires, yes, we seem to stay young. But we merely look young. On the inside, we are often ancient. And because of this long life, so many of us fall victim to our own cynicism. Be aware, the enemies of your wellness and youthfulness—which have nothing to do with venerated age—are a disengaged mind, body, heart and soul. Gather up your determination, and do not atrophy. You can be eternally youthful by caring for yourself – this does not mean attempting to reverse ageing. It means embracing life. It means exploring the potential of your body and what it can do. It means doing what you love, not necessarily what is age-appropriate. It means having an attitude of joyful investigation into life. It means, we see, again and again, that those with curiosity for adventure, and renewal, are those who are youthful, even into their most vintage of years. Do not waste your human youth. Do not waste any of this blessed life you have been given.

BLESSING: You are about to be rejuvenated and filled with energy and potential. You will look and feel very well, and your health will be vital. You will be very attractive and people will be drawn to your youthful free spirit and optimism.

CURSE: Tired, feeling old and worn. Feeling devalued by a society which reveres youthful appearances, wondering where your youth has gone, regrets about your younger years. Depleted energy.

WORKING WITH THIS CARD: Explore the blessings of the body and mind. It is time to discover what your body can do, and to instigate a transformation. It is time to give in to what you love, and to make it a larger part of your life. It is time to eat well, drink deeply of water and connect with new people. It is time to love being alive – for that drinking deep from the cup of life is the true fountain of youth.

2. Enlightenment

INSPIRATION, EPIPHANY, INNOVATION

LES VAMPIRES SPEAK: While a Vampire cannot walk in the sunlight, they are no strangers to various sources of light, and in fact adore candlelight, and the gentle glow of beeswax … they find that working and reading and contemplating by this light is soothing, reflective and comforting – especially when one is struggling to find answers to difficult dilemmas, as you are now. And so the answer will not come to you by daylight. It will come to you at night, and it will come to you by changing the source through which you expect enlightenment to arrive. In order to find an answer to the troubling issue at hand, you must first change the habits that have brought you this dilemma. You must switch the sources you go to for information. You must consider looking at the dilemma in a new and fresh way. And you ought best consider asking for assistance from one who has great experience with this kind of dilemma. You have until now, only sought justification as to why you should not have to endure this trouble – but there is an answer, and it is not in outrage, or denial, or avoidance. It is in seeking a fresh path through the forest, a light source unlike that of the sun, and advice from one who previously you were too proud to seek help from. The night has answers for you. Your shadows have the strengths you will need. Turn on a different source of light.

BLESSING: There will be a shift in your thinking, and a breakthrough regarding a difficult situation. You will be rethinking energy sources, and creating alternatives for power and energy. Independence and freedom of thought and thinking. Original stance, innovation and strokes of genius lead to enlightenment.

CURSE: Stuck on mental habits, trying to solve old problems in the same way, refusing to adopt new strategies and listen to advice that seems too "new" or "different" to you.

WORKING WITH THIS CARD: Make time to listen to your inner guidance, which will have bright ideas for you at this time. Attempt to move beyond habitual solutions to issues that feel entrenched. Dare to try something unusual and innovative! It might just work!

3. *Knowledge*

STUDY, LEARNING, EDUCATION

LES VAMPIRES SPEAK: Can you imagine what it would be like, to have a lifetime likely to stretch for one thousand years or more, to learn, to study and discover? For this is what we Vampires have – an eternity to study knowledge. The best of our kind take this miraculous opportunity to study, learn, and develop wisdom. And with this card, we can see that knowledge now seeks you. Ask yourself: What do you wish to learn? We can share what we study. When we learn, it is to fulfil our need to understand what is left of our human selves. We wish to reach a greater depth of understanding about the sensual life we lived – the cold we felt, and the way in which humanity has developed (your medicine, your technology), while your nature, and a part of ours, is left untouched, still primal. When you receive this message from us, it is time to consider the great treasure houses of wisdom that exist in your world. It is time to step beyond being "entertained" by the trivial sideshow of mainstream television and entertainment – to cease sleepwalking through your life, and become aware of the decreasing span of your precious mortal days. Ask yourself, what is it you wish to learn? A language? To paint? To think, and to think well? To use your gift of the human mind? Perhaps medicine, herbalism, and other helpful sciences attract you. It is time, we say then, to know you have greater capacity to study and learn. There may be a library near you. That library may come in the traditional form of beautiful tomes on shelf after shelf … ladders upon which you must climb … it may be a bookshop, which holds books you have never considered giving home to … and it may come in the form of a fellow being, who has stored so much knowledge, who is a library unto themselves.

It is time, to read, explore and learn more. Live, and die, and experience all you wish to – through the treasure of story and the treasury of knowledge that is books. This card can also indicate a need to ground your work, beliefs or knowledge with research. It is not always enough to simply "go within." Go within the souls of others too, and discover the incredible richness and potential of the human mind and expand yours too.

You have many more spans of time ahead of you, and there is knowledge waiting for you – you simply need to go to the library, and treat it as the magickal treasure trove of information that it is. Think not on how long it will take for you to learn – think of how joyous the knowledge will be, and how much achievement you will feel when it comes to you.

BLESSING: Know you are being called to become a student again, a true student, and follow in the long line of brilliant ones who learn so much, and then pass the knowledge on again. Books will figure greatly, as will reading, research and note taking. There may even be lectures – at which you could spy one of your undead friends radiating happiness that you are finally stepping into the full brilliance of your beautiful intelligence.

CURSE: You may feel that you are tired of study, or that you are too "something" … too old, too busy, too short of money, to open the books of knowledge and learn. But the library of the world's wisdom is now being opened to you, and you would do well to have a disciplined approach.

WORKING WITH THIS CARD: You will be divinely guided to find the right course to study, and the best books for you to read at this time. You are always learning, and this is what makes you wise!

4. *Ancient*

ANCESTRY, EGYPT, MAGICKAL INHERITANCE

LES VAMPIRES SPEAK: This ancient priestess sits amidst the bones of the past—she is the keeper of the secrets of the ancestors—and she raises the ancient vessel from which she will drink the blood, and consume again the knowledge of the past. For this you do too – you turn to the blood knowledge you have within you, over and over, to guide you, heal you, give you strength in times of sorrow. Even we, who are so often uncertain of how it is we can even walk the world, wonder, as we study more and more of human history – how we began. So it is for you too at this time. How did I begin, you wonder, where are my forbears from? What part does my history play in my present? What part does the history of the ancestors play in my present? And how will my past shape the future?

This card will often come up for humans who are adjusting to new information about members of their family – their heritage … the knowledge of what others have done, said, thought, felt, died of, been born into, is informing the present. You may be learning secrets about your family that have been kept for many years. And you will have with you a sense of the immortality of family lineage – that you are a part of the history of the planet, just as the plants and the trees are. Your family is the history of the plant – and it is time to acknowledge this and understand who you are, deep down, in the blood. And to find out which of this blood is wise, and which of this blood's influence can be overcome.

BLESSING: Family connections that lead you to greater knowledge of the self, and of how to work with the family members you know. There will be information that comes to you at this time that may surprise or disappoint – whatever the reaction, it is a gift to be able to know where you are from, and from whom the raw matter, the very cells of your being came.

CURSE: There may be a lack of knowledge about family and ancestry, a kind of dismissal that anything of the past matters, which leads to an unfortunate repetition. See the priestess, and see how she is working directly with ancestors of ancient times, and with their animal kin, and the ancient gods and goddesses. She may be very old—or she may be very young—but she is one who has a healthy respect for the ancient ones, the old ones, who are returning now, as never before.

WORKING WITH THIS CARD: Tap into ancestral energy, for it has much to offer you at this time. Simply take time to meditate, and see who comes to you.

5. *Nightmare*

PSYCHIC PROTECTION, SHIELD, BAD DREAMS

LES VAMPIRES SPEAK: Sometimes, we are at our most vulnerable when we sleep – or when we are attempting to sleep. This card speaks of the night which is restless, of the soul that cannot find the space in which to close their eyes and fully relax, whose dreams are creating agitation and distress, and who feels terror when knowing the darkness is falling, rather than the joy of the dark mother called night.

For the night can be a place of terror for many – where the past repeats, old wars are fought, deep wounds reopen, and betrayal of yesteryear is as fresh a cut as if it took place that day. For in the dreamscape there is no time as we know it when we are awake – we are at the mercy of the consciousness and that energy we have with us, and all the hauntings of the world are nothing to the damnation of the twilight hours.

If this is taking place for you or for another you care for, there is now a way for us to help you. This night-mare rider can enter your dreams. So fearless she is, and so fearsome her steed, that they will patrol the boundaries of your sleep, of your very dreams themselves. They will allow the gentler truths of your life to be recalled as you dream, and slowly, over time, the night will not hold such terror for you. Your dreams will become a safer place into which you can swoon each night, take your rest, and arise refreshed. At night there are special kinds of spirits who patrol—who hunt—the sleeping sensitives, and they can and do steal the energies of many, especially those whose energy is bright, open and innocent, and often those weakened by illness, stress or other imbalances. This Night Mare and her Dark Rider will protect you from these spirits. They will never hurt the one they are guarding—they are too honourable, too skilled, too powerfully devoted to their purpose for that —and they will ensure that no succubae, no limp ghost, no hungry denizen of the night can steal through the cracks in your auric field, and reap the energetic benefits of feeding on you. Dreams become beauty. Sleep becomes peace. Night is welcome, and the terrors of the past will change, when she rides forward, to guard your sleep.

BLESSING: Time to understand that at night, we can be vulnerable, and begin to work consciously towards lessening the fear of darkness, reclaiming healthy sleep, diminishing the reliance you may have on sleeping aids, dreams which disturb you will finally be understood and then depart, for good. A shift in your own energy will seal auric entrances to irritating and greedy little entities who are stealing your energy. You now have great support in seeking peaceful sleep. A great and beautiful human need.

CURSE: You may be living in fear, and unable to understand how you can make changes to your sleep patterns. It is time to get information on how to create better sleep. Your sleep patterns may be reversed, and you may be experiencing an almost nocturnal existence, which may be affecting your body's chemistry and magnetic field very strongly.

WORKING WITH THIS CARD:
Know you are protected and shielded when you sleep. You will soon be having nourishing, healing sleeps from which you awaken revived and ready for each day.

6. *Immortal*

THE CONSUMING FAMILY, PRESSURE OF PEERS

LES VAMPIRES SPEAK: For many humans, we have noticed that their blood – and adopted friendship families can exert a draining and consuming influence upon them. Whether it is that their affections are so strongly bound up within their families, that there is no affection to give elsewhere, or to others, or whether the family circle has closed so tight as to strangle a member, we know this thing we once had, and which many of you have—Family—can from time to time strangle the development of the soul and the being. If this card has come to you, we wish to show you a young vampiric maiden, one of our own, Lucrezia Borgia, whose famous family fed upon her youth and beauty to further their political ambitions. Her closeness with her brother, Cesare Borgia, in every way compromised the development of loyal affections elsewhere. The family of origin can be like this – for many humans. They can demand such great loyalty that you become entrenched in the family network, never moving beyond the ties of blood. This can be a diminishment of your potential, and we wish for you to consider that some of your beliefs have not been formed through your own independent experience, but have been fed to you, almost as mother's milk, or the blood we Vampires draw in from our prey. You are being eaten by the family, by its traditions, and by its needs. Through the hopes and dreams of the head of the family, be they female or male, there is an expectation that you will give up any individual wishes, and a belief that you ought indeed not have these, in order to further an empire or dynasty. In some families, this figure may be a narcissistic parent or sibling, who considers your existence as a source of energy to be used for their own satisfaction. Your own expression of self has never been a priority, and for you to find your own way will mean a struggle through the darknesses of guilt and fear of punishment. But the tribe you were born into now wants more than it gives, and it is time for you to find aspects of who you could be, if dreams were given space to grow within. It is time to move beyond their demands and needs, even if it is for a short time, and refresh the freedom you have as one human, rather than as a cluster of close-knit and similarly woven humans who share a surname, or an interest. You are more than your family. The family is not all. The group mind is a powerful thing. But for now, you must reassert your own individuality in healthy ways. For now, you must seek a form of freedom that comes from a separation, physical, emotional, mental, spiritual, from your family, their needs, their demands, the ties you have created yourself for a time.

BLESSING: The love and closeness of this group has given you a great sense of who you are, and what you are on earth to do. But we ask you now to shake up this situation, as it is now leading to a shadow of your soul development, and a stunting of your human growth. You are beyond the definitions of the family, or the peers of an adopted family, you are more than they say you are, more than they allow you to be, more than you have permitted yourself to be when in their orbit. It is time to separate.

CURSE: If you do not undertake a voyage of discovery into your own self, you will become enmeshed in the webs of the family life and a limited definition of self – and recall too, this can apply to friends who have strong beliefs about who you are, who you ought to be, and how you must do things. There is a great price to be paid for this approval – it is the consumption of the things within you that are budding, and have yet to flower. If you wish to be yourself, rather than simply a member of a group with a leader who is not you – it is time to explore the alternatives.

WORKING WITH THIS CARD: Remember you are your own person, and you can create your own life. You are free, and obligations can now fall away.

7. *Transmission*

SPREADING OF CONDITIONS, INFLUENCE, IMPACT

LES VAMPIRES SPEAK: There are those who cannot bear to be parted – and so, even if one has been infected with what you would call a negative (something that is likely to create difficulties and challenges in life, or even compromise life), some would rather share the negative experience than be parted by the possibility of two separate experiences. Thus we have a strange phenomenon. The deliberate adoption of behaviours and attitudes and sometimes even illnesses, almost as if they are infectious – even when they are not. You have names for this in your medical world – and your social scientists do work on this too. Who we spend our time with, who we share our lives with, is who we are very likely to become … we are special beings, even us, and we adapt and adopt – and become alike over time. It is as simple as observing that who you are with, who you spend your time with, who you choose to surround you, will have an influence on you. As your poet, John Donne said, "No man is an island." And so we sisters are here to tell you of the danger you are courting and the decision you must make.

For you are either influencing another – strongly, and they may make a life-changing decision simply to share life

43

with you more closely. They can't bear to be separate, and will draw closer to you through this. Or, another is influencing you – strongly, and you would rather endure what some call hell than be separated by diverging experiences.

For we sisters, the choice was made long ago. One of us was transformed, against her wishes. But the other could not be left behind, to live and die as a mortal, while the other watched. And our differing natures, growing further and further apart over the years – we could not bear to experience that. So we are together, for as long as we can sustain this form. Was this the right thing for us to choose? Should we have made another creature, deliberately, knowing the suffering it may bring?

Perhaps we should not have. But for us – facing our lives as separate beings, one a danger to the other, was not even a consideration. For you – your choice may be easier. Think, before the influence that need not be, takes a little of your soul away.

BLESSING: You will have someone to travel with on the journey you are undertaking. There will be friendship, laughter and the sharing of the experience.

CURSE: Feeling guilty for someone wanting to come with you. It is their choice, and their soul's journey. Do not deny them the gift of your company, simply because the road you share is tough.

WORKING WITH THIS CARD: Surround yourself with people and ideas that you wish to be influenced by. Create an amazing support network.

8. *Seduction*

ALLURE, DESIRE, MANIPULATION

LES VAMPIRES SPEAK: This beautiful bed is the place where someone greeted their unspoken desire, and where they met their end. It is the place to which so many of you are drawn, even when you know the outcome may be dangerous. This card comes to you now to warn you, empower you, and ask you to heed. The one who knows what it is you want, has a plan for you … and that plan involves their own satisfaction. There is one about you who understands very deeply what people desire – and most especially what you desire. It is not so simple and crass as sexual satisfaction, or a kind of food, or even a job or status in life you are being offered; it is the deep feeling that you are understood, accepted and desired for who you are. But it is a truth that this person who is now seducing you, is doing so with every kind of ability to stifle and inhibit your life force. This is not to say that you must look about you now with suspicion of all people – you must simply become aware of your desires, and your vulnerabilities. This card is a call to self-knowledge. To understand that when you are called to the beautiful bed, you may be drained, and you may even die to a part of yourself. For you will come to know that the love that has been offered to you, has been for the satisfaction of another. If you do go to the bed of the Vampire, you will leave a part of yourself there. Someone about you is ready to seduce you. If you choose to be seduced, they will have what they want, and you will lose more than you know. Be careful.

BLESSING: You are now able to discern much more clearly between people who are healthy for you, and people who you would do well to avoid. You are no longer feeling guilty for saying "no" to attractive advances.

CURSE: It is time to reassess a friendship, or the kinds of people and situations you find attractive. Are you inviting unwelcome dramas and situations into your life?

WORKING WITH THIS CARD: You are able to resist unhealthy advances from manipulative people at this time. You are no longer available for others to make use of!

9. *Creator*

CATALYST, MAKER, MOTHER, FATHER

LES VAMPIRES SPEAK: As vampiric ones, we can create a new life – we become Makers, and so we are akin to the alchemists of your history, who tried again and again to make life. Now you call them scientists and they merge cells, transform bodies, change people's shapes, repair great injury, change destiny. Sometimes this is wonderful. And sometimes, it is most destructive. Of whom do we speak with this card? The destructive geniuses amongst you. They are vampiric ones to us, the ones who convince you that your beauty, your beautiful vulnerable unique humanity, is not enough. You are being sold a new religion, that of conformity … and each time one conforms, a soul is partially lost – for your soul is held within the nucleus of your cells, within each one of them. You are the Creator of yourself. While you may not create Vampires, or birth a new life from the Blood, you are still a creator – each day with your thoughts, actions and decisions you create anew the form your natural energies and soul will take. This is what we wish to say to you now. You can recreate yourself. You may choose to live in the light, or in the dark. We Vampires have a choice too – we must live in the dark, but we can still be agents of the light, a candle in the dark, with our illumined skin and radiant blood shining from within.

When you receive this card you are being reminded of your responsibility as a creator – you have created an idea, perhaps even given birth to a new one of your kind, just as this Vampire alchemist has created the tiny deer she will feed with a vial of transforming blood. You are the vessel through which new life and ideas are born – and life, the new ones, the small creatures you have about you are looking to you for so much guidance. As a creator, you are responsible for those you make. You must see through the time after they are born. You must nurture the young ones, be they ideas or projects or real, living beings. You must also teach them, and train them, and let them know how to survive. You must be sure they have those essential skills only you can teach them – and teach them well. You must also love them, despite their imperfections. You must find within you that great reservoir of love that even we Vampires never lose, that human part of us that never leaves us, and keeps us ensoulled.

When we create a new one, they struggle and are often confused and in pain. 'Tis the same for your new ventures and children – they will encounter the pain and struggle of newness. They will have a terrible vulnerability. It is your mission, your honour, and your duty—yes, that foolish, old-fashioned word—to help them through this time. And with the doing of this, you will become again more than you were.

BLESSING: You have much to teach, and if you must create, and you must, you are required by laws that bind together the entire natural and unnatural world to see through until you have shared what you can. It is time to create, and to share with your creations your knowledge. It is time in short, to be a Maker, a parent, a mature being.

CURSE: It is not easy to care for our offspring – they grow in ways we do not like. They have traits we did not predict they would have. They require time and effort, emotions and even pain. They take a great deal, and they feed from us – just as this deer takes the very blood of her vampiric creator. In the feeding, though, we bring real life, real lifeblood to all. Whether this is a metaphor for you and the sheer lifeblood you must give projects, or the milk your baby takes from you, feed what you have given birth to. As a Maker, you will find joy and pain in this.

WORKING WITH THIS CARD: You have a creative spirit, and the ability to bring to life a wonderful new project. This will bring you wonderful responsibilities and opportunities. Don't hesitate or delay! This is part of your sacred purpose!

10. *Her Last Day in the Light*

UNEXPECTED ENDINGS, SURPRISE CHANGES, SUDDEN SHIFTS

LES VAMPIRES SPEAK: What, you may wonder, is this Angel so clearly defined by daylight doing here, amidst we ones who walk the dark path, and who are committed to assisting you to understand your blessings and enrich the great wonder of the human life you have been given? She is here, for she is about to become one of us, and this image depicts her last day amidst those who walk under daylight. There are many times in your human life when you walk for the last time in a circumstance or situation, which you take very much for granted. But we are here to share with you news both good and bad: the news that a time is coming to an end, and a great source of security may be about to finish for you. It will soon be your turn to experience a hardship that only you can bear, and become heroic in the undertaking. There is no cause for you to fear, though being human, you will fear. It is time to understand more of what you have avoided and what circumstance soon to come to you will teach you. You will not lose anything that you cannot bear – although it is a sacrifice and it shall be difficult, and at times, you will struggle. But this ending must take place for you to come to even greater illumination at a later time, and for the angelic nature within you to grow, you must endure something that will temper you, as the finest sword of the Archangel Michael. You will become again one who walks in the miracle of the light, of colour, of the creatures who live amongst the rays of light that stream from the noble sun. But soon, you will go into the night of your soul, and you will confront parts of yourself that cannot be seen by the light of the sun – they can only be found as they shine in the dark. So soon, shine … but shine in the dark time. You will have courage, and you will return one day to the song of the birds, to the hope of the robin, to the faith you may have lost for a time. It will be yours again. And if you are already within this dark time, and this card emerges – then soon, you will walk again into the light. You will emerge. And all about you will be the Miracle of Day, of Light, after the great darkness.

BLESSING: Prepare for change. If you are currently in darkness, and your soul is weary and aching, take hope: you will soon emerge into the light again — a risen one. Even if the past lies in ruins, the miracle of life will once more be the greatest blessing to behold. The simplest companions of the day will bring you the greatest joys.

CURSE: Being unprepared for change means we can be shocked and disrupted by the unexpected. But this is also a great time to test your skills and your beliefs – you will be able to handle this change, and move through it with grace, no matter how difficult it may seem.

WORKING WITH THIS CARD: Know that change is a healthy part of life, and even the most difficult and harsh shifts in our lives can create the perfect conditions for our own development and transformation.

11. *Death Rites*

SAYING GOODBYE, FORMAL OCCASION, HONOURING LIVES

LES VAMPIRES SPEAK: For many beings, the reality of death seems to be the ultimate cruelty—the Vampire that steals the life from so many—and without, it seems, any order or reality. For death it is true visits us all, whether we are young, or old, or healthy, or suffering … for all of us, beast and beauty, there is a time for the end to come. But there are angels of death, appointed by the universe to help us move from one side, to the next … and to avoid staying in between, without moving on, transforming. For the soul who dies well, who has a good death, there is a transformation through the realms that divide the living from the dead.

For this to take place, the angel of death does not only come to assist the soul, but they assist with the ones left behind. And what comforts those who remain on the earth are rites, ways to say goodbye, honourings and reverence, and memories and mirth. It may be time for you to consider those who have gone from you, or who may go – and know how you would honour them, and remember them, and send them on their way. What rites will you prepare – ones to help carry the soul into the arms of the angel of death? Consider what will comfort you when you are on your way too – know that it is not morbid to contemplate the ending of this mortal time for you. There is so much beyond that last breath, that last glimpse of light of the sun – so the angel of death assures us. But her job is to stay in the borderlands – she knows little of heaven, for it is a memory. She knows of humans, and of the creatures of the earth, and their souls, and of taking them across the veil. If you are deeply grieving, and in pain, this card signals that you will soon receive divine support, relief and assistance.

Wills and legal documents may be about to enter your life when this card comes to you – consider too the legacy you will leave when you have departed. Consider your children, and their children. Consider the wellbeing of the animals and plants, your library, your keepsakes, your little treasures. Begin the journey of safeguarding these now. They will not matter to you beyond this life, it is true, not as they do now, nor in the same manner. As you enter your next lifetime they may not even be recalled at all. But those who you may leave will know them, and know you through them. Let yourself live on, and know who will keep your memory bright as a candle, and you will look from time to time, and be glad, and be able to send messages of comfort.

BLESSING: Honouring the ones who we have loved and who have left can be a beautiful way to come to terms with their absence, and a way to help their soul make the transition to their new life beyond the veil. Evidence of life beyond death.

CURSE: Feeling that death is final, and losing hope in the purpose of life. Trapped by grief.

WORKING WITH THIS CARD: It's time to work with any fear you may have around death and dying, and transform this through preparation, contemplation of your legacy, and considering the interactions you have had with deceased loved ones.

12. *Call for Help*

REACH OUT, NEED FOR BACK-UP, ADMIT YOUR NEEDS

LES VAMPIRES SPEAK: Often, you humans have an unerring ability to sense when we are around. When there is danger. When there is something not quite right. Something amiss. And yet over and over you smother this feeling, this intuitive gift you all have. It may have been educated out of you. It may have been taken, or suppressed. You may have been taught to feel ashamed of it. It may also have been so indulged and over stimulated that it is now a lazy muscle, a nonsense sense. But at this time, you are able to discern when there is a shift in the atmosphere. When something is about or around you. It is pre-sentience, and it is clear. And when this card comes to you, we say, your senses are correct, they are natural, and they are good, and it is time to share this feeling with a trusted friend or person in authority who can help. It is time to remove yourself from an atmosphere of danger, to understand that you are not weak for seeking help, and that further confirmation is not required. All you need to do is ask for assistance, and it will come. No more looking over your shoulder. No more doubting your very real, very worthwhile sixth sense. Trust it. And take steps to make yourself safe and comfortable. Remove untrustworthy people. Be cautious in your dealings. Lift your shields, and stand with an ally and friend. Do not allow your innocence to create a dangerous moment for you. For someone is waiting for you to drop your guard. Do not let it be now. Dare to take your own premonition seriously.

BLESSING: It is wonderful to have foreknowledge of when you need to work with protection and shielding. This will help you immensely!

CURSE: Feeling hurt and attacked, weakened and like a victim.

WORKING WITH THIS CARD: Protect yourself by clearing your space, and working with a shielding technique that works for you. Simply visualise yourself completely surrounded by a sphere-shaped field of soft white energy. Within this, you are safe, and protected. Nothing harmful can reach you through this. Affirm you are safe and well, and take steps to strengthen your body, mind and spirit. Dare to try something unusual and innovative! It might just work!

13. *Primal*

CONNECTING DEEP WITHIN, SACRED DANCE, INSTINCT

LES VAMPIRES SPEAK: When we move, we say so many things about ourselves. The way we hold our bodies, the way we inhabit them, and the way we speak with our physical selves, we are communicating. Our energy is within our bodies, and it reaches out through us, and we speak through our form. As modern people, we forget this – and we tend to move as though our minds are living a separate life to our bodies.

When we dance, we are asked to become our deeper, older, more animistic self, when dancing is at its best. When dancing is at its worst, it is a messy, embarrassing, self-conscious affair, which says to the world that you find the business of being within a body a less than magnificent gift. Dance is an expression of health, personality, and of your nature – your natural self. There is a difference between when humans dance and when creatures do … when humans dance, and when they dance deeply, from a place where they are unselfconscious and as if they are unwatched, or care not if they are watched – they are deeply, incomparably beautiful. When they dance with their whole souls, they are primal … and when humans often hear that word and let it fall from their lips, they feel that to be primal is simply to be aggressive, to roar and to scream, to be raw and unaffected …

But you represent this primal quality for us when you dance and we enjoy nothing more than seeing you come to life through movement, than when you feel through your senses and speak to us through your senses, and when you fail to be trapped and domesticated. The being dancing in this image is a wild one, primal, ancient, feminine … she is one of us, and yet reconnects with her humanity and beauty through the joy of movement, and the memory of the body.

BLESSING: Your body loves movement and is asking you to experience the primal joy of dancing freely, wildly and with every cell in your body alight with joy.

CURSE: You may feel self-conscious when moving or dancing, and feel as though you are observing yourself from the outside in, watching and judging yourself. Time to let this go and feel the music in your body!

WORKING WITH THIS CARD: There is a beautiful untamed part of your soul. Let it stay free, and find expression in the world through dance.

14. *Compassion*

EMPATHY, SYMPATICO, KINDNESS

LES VAMPIRES SPEAK: There are times in our life when circumstances, and people, and what we see have a certain horror to them. It is the horror of being unable to believe that there is such cruelty, and malice, and injustice in the world. Each day, if we allow ourselves, we expose our minds, and our hearts and energies, to events that hold enough tragedy within them for us to suffer pain on behalf of other humans, animals, and all the fellow creatures we share this planet with. We children of the night know this suffering too, and sometimes cannot bear to stand it a moment longer. We have no more forbearance at times, and that is when we step forward, and carry those who are suffering so very deeply. Within this card are elements of your great beliefs – your beautiful Christ, God made flesh, at his moment of being taken down from the cross, at that moment, released from suffering. In this way, we want you to know that all the suffering you see, all the hardship you can observe, is unendurable for us, too. So we must step forward, and even God does not refuse help, even when it comes from one who many would claim to be the opposite of all they consider to be good. When this card appears to you, know that even the unlikeliest hearts hold compassion, and sometimes, they cannot bear the suffering about them, any more than you can. And they become an ally, comforting those who have fallen, who are unable to rise and take steps towards the rebirth of their own life. This deep compassion means that they will refuse to take comfort, or exit their lives of hardship, because they know that where they are, they can do most good. And there is much good within us, and so much good within you. If you have fallen, you will be caught up in strong arms, and helped and tenderly nurtured. You will be treated with respect, although at this time you may be unconscious of this fact. And the one who will gather you up, when you have unravelled, when you are fallen, is not the one who you thought would come to your aid.

BLESSING: This is an opportunity to change your mind about who has compassion within their heart, and who is a caring being. For the great nurturing tenderness and yearning to ease the misery in the world through being kind to you at this time will come through an unexpected source. And there is great goodness in their act, although you may never have thought of them as one, or the kind, who cares.

CURSE: You may fear that accepting help will mean you are judged as weak. When you accept the help that will be offered, you will become stronger, and it is that strength that will be seen most clearly.

WORKING WITH THIS CARD: This card could also herald a time when you seek to do volunteer work, help others in unexpected situations … and become, in some way, the embodiment of the Holy human expression that is the most beautiful compassion.

15. *Reason*

LISTEN TO ADVICE, THINK CLEARLY, INTELLECT

LES VAMPIRES SPEAK: I am the one who comes to you now so you can see clearly! You feel others have had problems in this area, but if you simply think positively and send out waves of love the way will be cleared. But no, this is not how this particular power works, my friend. There is an obstructive force around you at present, one that will not allow you to pass, unless you strictly meet all criteria. This force, in the form of a person, or institution, or corporation requires you to do everything that is required to pass through the gates. How do I know this? I am one of them, and have been one of them, and will continue to be the gatekeeper for many activities. I am a Queen, and I choose who enters the gateways of immortality in my realm, and for all those who dare climb the path to my lair, there are many who are turned away … and they are the fortunate ones.

So, although you may consider yourself to be more charming, more well-liked, able to convince others, and worthy of inclusion, there is tedious paperwork and criteria that must be met – and we Vampires have this too. You must do everything perfectly, if you wish to pass the test, and gain what it is you seek.

This card is likely to come up for you mortals when dealing with large companies and government institutions … once it was the Church who controlled … now it is the people with their pens and paper, their digital records, their officious ways … This card will come to you at tax time, or when you must take pen to paper and fill out a form of endless length. I am the Vampire who warns you of contracts, and who asks you to read, and read again, the agreements you sign. Do not consider yourself different or better than others – for when it comes to matters like these, we are all subject to laws that are tedious at worst, punishing at times, and cruel at others. How cruel, you may wonder? Think of the immigrant, waiting for the signature so they can live in a new land. Think of the mother, who must rely on the form going to the right department so food can be found for her child. The list goes on and on—there is a cruelty to the faceless conformity of bureaucracy—and to the negligence that can stifle your plans, and sometimes even threaten your very future. Take care. Be aware. And do everything, as if you were writing with your very blood, and it was your soul you were selling.

BLESSING: Your mind is powerful, and will be used for your soul's highest purpose. Accept excellent advice, and see the results this can bring.

CURSE: Fear of accepting advice that seems almost too sensible. A belief that "nothing is easy." Panicking and being overwhelmed with details and paperwork. Feeling you have no one to turn to.

WORKING WITH THIS CARD:

Time to sit calmly down, clear your mind, then begin to work your way through the details of a dilemma. There is a person about you who is able to advise you – please ask them for their assistance, and listen and act when that good advice is given.

16. *The Call of the Night*

DARING, ADVENTURE, EXCITEMENT

LES VAMPIRES SPEAK: You have of late fallen into patterns that are soothing in their regularity. You know what to expect, and when to expect it. You are surrounded by love and acceptance, and you are widely loved and applauded. You are content. You are comfortable, and have no real reason to become otherwise. Is what you have achieved not the pinnacle of human experience? To live, and to live without fear or being tested?

I say to you now, I was once like you. And then, the night and her darkness called me. I changed, and I left behind the world of daylight, and for a time I travelled from my loved ones, although some chose to travel with me. I departed from all that I knew in so many ways, and in doing so, I became more perfectly myself than if I had stayed in that perfectly still, comfortable place. For in the testing, I was reborn. For in the challenge, I was forged. And in the loneliness, I came to know myself. This time is one which I can only partake of, truly, alone. And for you, you fear leaving the comfort zone. You prefer all that is known. But I tell you, that with this card comes the Call of the Night, and of her wild creatures … and you are about to leave that place of warmth, that cosy, restrictive, dulling cocoon, and step into a colder, harsher, more raw place. What it will teach you, and offer you, is more valuable and strange than you can imagine. You will be thrust out of that place you have called home – and into a world of movement, colour, drama and some ferocity. You will make friends who respect you and challenge you. You will be disagreed with, and you will fight to survive at times. But the adventure will leave you feeling more alive, your every sense tingling, more than ever before.

BLESSING: Attraction, stimulated, daring, unexpected, thrill, danger, change in circumstance, drawn to the occult, unknown, wish to understand, experimentation, challenges and tests.

CURSE: Routine thinking, rut, conditioned to obey, lazy, dull, asleep, bland, insipid, cowardly, unchallenged, safety, tedious. Apathy, indifference.

WORKING WITH THIS CARD: Time to step beyond the places and people where you feel safe. This is a time to stretch your wings and to seek out new friends, experiences and people. You will find so much if you dare to explore!

17. *The Past a Prison*

BITTERNESS, GRUDGE, REFUSAL TO LET GO

LES VAMPIRES SPEAK: Miss Havisham is a character from Charles Dickens' most beautiful novel, *Great Expectations*. She is a truly vampiric creature, who devours the young lives she encounters to avenge a great and devastating betrayal she experienced long ago, in her treasured, nurtured past. For Miss Havisham was "left at the altar" as they once said in the days of long ago – and her entire life is now a devotion, a frozen testament to that horrible, wounding moment. She has trained her one and only charge, a young woman, to devour the lives of the young men she encounters, by having them fall in love with her, and then leaving them, again and again, gaining revenge for the old woman in her doom. Bitterness is a most terrible thing. Even those who claim they are healed often nurse a great grudge within them. Others claim that to forgive is to deny that they were ever wronged. But to refuse to forgive can create a bitter destiny, like that of Miss Havisham. Each day she reminds herself of all her hurt, and then forces her own personal bitterness and pain into hearts innocent and open. She wounds them with her warning, without them having done her any harm. Beware those who are bitter, who have a special moment of hurt that they bring up to you over and over again. Be wary of those who speak ill of someone who has long been out of their life, who want you to inherit their burden. It is not yours to carry. And it is their choice to keep carrying the burden they complain of.

We are reminded of people who wish to avenge family members for harm done in other generations, those who train the young and the innocent to carry a grudge and a hurt that they would otherwise be free of. We know that these creatures are more vampiric than any who would drink your life-force once, and move on. If you are one who was young and innocent, but who has been turned through guilt to a path of vengeance, be aware. You can feel compassion for the hurt someone has suffered without becoming them, without your life being consumed by an event you never experienced. The monstrous and dreadful selfishness of such humans is tragic – not only for those they infect with their bitterness, but for themselves, for all the long lives they live, steeping in their own sour energy.

Why have you received this card? We warn you now, of the motives of another who insists on telling their tragic story to you, over and over, until you have lost part of your soul to them, and wish to defend them. Heed our message: this is not your battle to fight, nor your story to live. You have your own path, and you will have your own tragedies. Yes, you can support another, with time, your care, and lend a hand. But they wish none of these things—they wish your full consumption by their story—and they will condemn you if you do not immerse yourself in their long past issue. Watch – and see if they wish you to re-enact their issues.

And if so – then beware, and do your best to live your story, and to distance yourself from this one, who will ask you to deny your own story, and live out their own, again and again, until you forget your self, and become a shadow of who you were always intended to be. Do not make someone else's past your prison.

BLESSING: You now have a chance to free yourself from the sadness and misery of another, and to set a wonderful example of how to live freely, without bitterness and regret.

CURSE: Your kindness and desire to help may be creating a situation where you are hearing a great deal of negativity. This is having an impact on your energy. Please take steps to remove this influence, and to listen less.

WORKING WITH THIS CARD: Find those who have suffered, and who have moved on – for they are the great hearts, the ones who have the most to teach, and who have the greatest souls. Find the ones who have not just forgiven, but who have taken their hurt and put it into constructive purpose, and helped many others.

18. *Anti-Hero*

MAVERICK, RISK-TAKER, RULE-BREAKER

LES VAMPIRES SPEAK: You are doing a good thing. But it is unlikely you will wear the garland of the hero, or be recognised for any real contribution to the greater good. You are not the kind of being who people acknowledge, and it has been this way for a long time. This is because most people are trained to recognise what looks good – from appearances, the kind of jobs people have, and the way you humans even walk and talk. And the person, the human being you are, is something that cannot be identified and classified simply, but the truth is that you have done a very good thing. You are a safe person, a good one, we can sense this from you, and we wish to acknowledge the valour and the brightness that surrounds you. The deed that you have done will not be recognised as soon as you would wish, but the impact it has will ripple out through the energy of the world, and in return, you will be noticed by many, many who also will never quite fit in, or be recognised despite the good they do. Do not take this to heart. Do not allow this to ever prevent you from doing what you are urged to do – and do not allow all the moments where you have been unlike your best self to define you. You are a mixture of what people call good and bad, and what is taking place now is a kind of working your way through what you feel you must do to rebalance the ledger in life. This does not mean you will ever receive an award, or be offered a hand to shake. You may even fail to be recognised again and again. But now, we see you. And so many others see you too. You will find that creatures who are less socialised will trust you and come to you – the young, animals, creatures whose senses are more alert, and who rely on feeling rather than what they see. You are a truly beautiful soul in parts – and yes, you have done things that have been called wrong, and were. But humans are complex, and they enjoy calling you wrong, for they then feel superior, and they draw attention to their supposed goodness. All are the sum of their actions, and their choices within their circumstances. Even the roughest and most humble among us can become the hero, and those who are greatest and most seen to do good, often are glorying in their own virtues. Do not fear. You are a walker of the night, and yet, your time will come. You will inspire love. You are more than those who cannot see you, say you are. Their voices are empty. Your life, although strange, is full.

BLESSING: You are displaying to humans who are thinking too much in boxes, with labels, that those who do good are not always going to fit a cultural stereotype.

CURSE: To feel neglect, to feel resentment that others receive the glory for your deeds. Perhaps know you have chosen this way in order to remain an outsider, so you need not enter into groups in the same way. You are in a stage where you are working very strongly with your unique energy and power.

WORKING WITH THIS CARD: Your individuality is a gift from the Divine. You are the only person on the planet like you. You truly are here for a purpose, and you truly are needed here. No matter how modest this purpose, do it well, with all your heart, and there will be no more loneliness.

19. Maenad

MADNESS, ECSTATIC RITUAL, ENERGY RELEASE

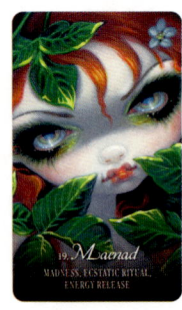

LES VAMPIRES SPEAK: Maeneds are the female priestesses of the God Dionysus, maddened by the fruits of the vine, and given the space of ritual, they descend into a ritual ecstasy, where an orgy of carnal delights, instability, frenzied dance, and gluttony are all allowed and celebrated. Within that space, the divine madness we all have—including you—is given expression, and exhausts itself, relatively safely. When she comes to you in this card, it is for you to now find a safe space to do what you have considered to be unsafe, in a safe and protected way. What does this mean? You may be longing to be free, wild and to let loose … to cast off the chains and find expression in dancing, sex, parties, and intoxication … and she comes to you now, this creature who will devour you if you do not find a way to safely express these urges. For that is vampiric—the urge to express the divine madness that will erode your soul if you repress it any longer—and that is when the vampiric maenad can tear you to pieces. That is when addiction can find you. This is when over-indulgence can stake its claim on your soul through your physical form. This maenad is watching you now, eyes brimming with poison, ready to infect you, if you do not begin to rediscover the beautiful madness of life in your own way. If you do not now begin to have some dance, some joy, some loss of the self-consciousness you battle with each day, she will find you, and her leaves will poison you, even as they delight you. It is time for joy to be lived through you. It is time for madness. It is time to drink the nectar of love making, wine, laughter to the point where your belly hurts … it is time.

BLESSING: It is safe for you to give way to feelings of intense bliss and happiness, even excitement. Feeling deeply and allowing yourself to be swept up in the rapture is a beautiful thing for you to experience at this time! It is safe to let this happen under the current circumstances!

CURSE: A fear that divine madness will be permanent, that there is a short distance between the bliss of the maenad and insanity. Keeping yourself on such a tight leash that your repressions rule you, and are therefore expressed in unhealthy ways.

WORKING WITH THIS CARD: Dancing, going out, and indulging in ritual that gives you a safe escape valve for your wild urges needs to be created now – or else you may find the virtues you have worked so hard to establish eroding. And if you do things in a sacred way, there will be a kind of beauty to the madness. No more control. Find a safe place. Find the safe people. And go wild, just for a little while within the temple you create. Do this, and transcendence will follow – that loss of self leads to the uniting with the Great Spirit, the great soul of this world and beyond, and when you go to this place, and drink of the Holy Grail of life, you will return replenished, whole, and fully returned. This will bring strength.

20. *Redemption*

ABSOLUTION, FORGIVENESS, PENANCE

LES VAMPIRES SPEAK: Vampiric creatures in myth and legends are rarely sorry for their actions ... but you do not know how sorry we are for so much of what we have done. Penitence is a kind of healing, so when this card comes to you, you are being shown clearly that you need to feel the relief of saying sorry. This penitence is not made to burden or punish the self, but to relieve the self from the negative impact of imbalanced action, thoughts and words. It hurts us when we hurt another. It is a form of self-abuse to indulge a momentary urge for spite, or selfishness, or greed, because you will pay for that, over and over. And you resist the apology, you do, for we have seen it. You fight the need to say, "I can do better." For you can. You truly can. And to admit to such is not to take blame or be made wrong, for anyone wishing to do this to you is not a pure soul. But for you to recognise a misdeed, and to affirm you are better than that, by saying "I am sorry," this is a humble, beautiful, strengthening thing. To say sorry, is to be redeemed from the self-hatred, the judgment, and the silent criticism that otherwise repeats throughout your mind. Be what you are: sorry. Repent, but do not punish yourself. Be sorry for the right reasons

– this is not 'sorry' for being human, for loving, for making a mistake. It is sorry for hurting another who expected that you be your best self. And what that best self is, is what you must decide, and aim to become.

BLESSING: Being able to be sorry, to say sorry, and take responsibility will lift any burdens you may be carrying from your shoulders.

CURSE: The blame and self-punishment you are currently inflicting upon yourself cannot make amends. Whatever we hold within can poison us.

WORKING WITH THIS CARD: It is time to be open about your remorse, and to let what has been secret to be said.

21. *Thirst*

CRAVING, COMPULSION, OBSESSION

LES VAMPIRES SPEAK: You are currently craving something with such a great thirst that it is dominating your thoughts and feelings and you can think of hardly anything else. Thirst can be wonderful when that which you long for, yearn for, is healthy and wise – but in this case, the thirst is for the kind of experience you know will have life-changing consequences. For with us, the thirst we experience is not just for the blood, the drink that sustains us, it is for the stream of humanity and the song of life and beautiful warmth that runs through the blood. So too for you: what you thirst for is very close to becoming an addiction, or an obsession which draws you away from what makes you, you. If it is a person you thirst for, their touch, their love, or if it is a substance, know that this thirst is exerting a powerful force, even close to a control. There may be an addiction, or an addictive way of thinking and feeling working its way into your life. We wish to direct your consciousness to this thirst, and ask you to question its source – what is it the thirst craves? Can it be satisfied? Or are you simply compelled to search and drink again and again. Know that some thirsts can be satisfied in ways that are in tune with your personality, your 'self' this time, all manifestations of your essence and soul. And others will steal you further and further away from your true self.

BLESSING: The thirst will lead you to know more about yourself and how far you go to quest for something you want. You could encounter a way through to self-knowledge. But consider too that what you thirst for you may never find. Many of we children of the night thirst more for the humanity we have been separated from in so many ways than we thirst for the blood of the same.

CURSE: This thirst—for knowledge, for a person, for fulfilment, for lust, for ecstasy and the vanishment of pain through experiences or foods, drugs or alcohol that distract you from the pains you no longer wish to feel—dominates you. The thirst is so strong that it is taking over your life force and your will. You are being consumed. It is time to assert yourself, your true self once again.

WORKING WITH THIS CARD: It is possible to reclaim your life force, your will. Even we Vampires learn to do this, and after years of practice, we no longer need to give in to our lust for life and your lifeblood. Your desire is driving you – be sure of where it is taking you, and whether it is increasing your ability to live fully alive, or whether it is dragging you into a seductive soul sleep from which you may struggle to awake. It is time to be open and honest with yourself about what has power over you. Take steps to reclaim your power, and listen to your guidance, being sure to follow the voice within that wants you express your own power in safe and healthy ways.

22. Outsider

MISFIT, LONER, WANDERER

22. Outsider
MISFIT, LONER, WANDERER

LES VAMPIRES SPEAK: And yet, the distance between you and others gives you a unique and valuable perspective. You, like us, feel estranged from the human world at the moment we find you with this card. It is as if a glass separates you from others, and their world. You look at the lives of others, and there is a sense of mild regret at how distant it all seems. You feel unable to find the true meaning in anyone else's experience, and you cannot relate to what so many people care about – you do not care who wins the latest reality TV show! You do not know what it is you will do for the rest of your human days. You do not understand why so many people wish to be esteemed for their clothing or their cars, or the title of their job. You cannot express these feelings to most people, and if you are blessed, as we so rarely are for fleeting moments, with a true sense of companionship, the loneliness, the isolation, and that sense of having no home ends for just a little while. But for now, you feel an outsider, looking ever inwards, but not feeling a part of any community, or group, or even any family. At this time, strange as it can be, disorienting as it can be, you are wondering about your human-ness, if indeed you really belong to this great, thriving, greedy, enormous, wise and childish family called the human race. This estrangement is current, but it is not eternal. Still, there will always be something of the orphan child about you, even if you have never suffered the abandonment so many have. You simply are different, and you have yet to find your own kind. And the truth is that when you do find your own kind, you and they may only be able to be with each other in unusual, unconventional ways, or for shorter lengths of time.

BLESSING: You have been given the opportunity to find your own way and to see the world from a unique perspective. This will give you great creative, artistic and spiritual opportunities.

CURSE: Being outside the tribe. Searching for home. Lack of comfort.

WORKING WITH THIS CARD: Accepting the outsider's position for now, you can observe, and watch, and see, and record. This will make you a valuable writer, artist, teacher. Your unique perspective will be greatly valued.

23. *Free Will*

SOVEREIGNTY, INDEPENDENCE, FREE SPIRIT

LES VAMPIRES SPEAK: One of the ironies of the vampiric life is that many of us who have become this unnatural, yet very much alive creature did not choose to become this way. We were turned, created, transformed, and often against our will. And so we wish to speak to you through this card of the sacred nature of free will, of consent. There are those who walk among you who many call witches, and within their laws is one which is to do with the consent and consciousness that must come with the casting of a spell. This casting that we do, this spell of the most ancient kind, must be carried out with consent, or because of circumstances that impel this transformation. Your free will, and the free will of others is sacred. If one is taken and transformed, a dreadful bond is created, and one which must be paid for, most often with pain. For to transgress the wishes of another is against the laws we have developed to keep us from falling too deeply into an abyss of depravity and cruelty. If you have had something occur against your will, you will feel something of your soul's vitality draining from you, for the soul needs its blood, its chi, nwyfre, prana, too. It may be unseen, but the angels can glimpse it, as can those of you with the preternatural sight.

Free will is as sacred as a sacrament in the Church, and to you, this is very important at present. If one has stolen fragments of your soul through the imposition of their will upon your own, strengthen your Will at this time. Do not go with the flow, as they say – for this is an energy imposed by culture, or by another soul, who loves to have the energy of those who follow them at their disposal.

BLESSING: You know now that to do something against the free will of another – to withhold or to connive to take from another what they need to make a full decision, is a kind of sin. And when one steals this right from another, a bond is developed between the two. Perhaps not immediately, but a reckoning will be made, and a debt will be paid. You are considering how best to respect this right, while achieving what it is you wish for in this lifetime. Simply respect this law and all that comes to you will bring great blessings.

CURSE: The negativity that is created when there is deliberate and thought-out interference with the free will of another is not to be taken lightly. And of this we say, be prepared for the link that comes, and the day the cord of energy will suddenly tug at you. Do as you will, as the wise sages say, but harm ye none. Something will be taken – but do it for selfish reasons, for the delight in thwarting another's will, manipulate and deceive … and it will haunt you, as surely as any ghoul in a decaying corpse yard. Do not allow this taint to become yours.

WORKING WITH THIS CARD: Remind yourself of your own dreams and desires, of the purpose that has asked to be expressed through you. Activate your ability to say "yes" and "no" without guilt, without fear. It is safe and easy for you to express and act upon your free will.

24. *Love Conquers All*

ENDURING LOYALTY, ETERNAL LOVE, LASTING COMMITMENT

24. *Love Conquers All*
ENDURING LOYALTY, ETERNAL LOVE,
LASTING COMMITMENT

LES VAMPIRES SPEAK: Some love endures only until a change comes to visit. And then that love, that connection, the friendship can dissolve. Some friendships and connections are strong and healthy, only to die due to neglect, or because one partner shifts an alliance to another. But in the heart of these creatures, these faithful ones, we can see a love and a commitment that truly is enduring. For we have experienced it, just as this new Vampire is experiencing it within this image. From one lifetime to the next, through transformation, they will come to greet her. They know she is changed. They can sense her difference. But they are hers, and she is theirs, and that bond is unbreakable, until true death takes them away from each other, and even then, the love endures through memory and the presence that lingers after death. This young Vampire does not know how fortunate she is yet – she may not even know how very much she has changed, transformed as she is, awakened and alive to her Vampire sense she has become. But for her, these wolves are her friends. They were her dearest ones, and now, that bond will grow even stronger, as they will remind her of her human self, and of her compassion. They will also teach her to survive, to hunt, to be wild. And though she has never been less like them, they are all now creatures of the night, and hunters. A new love out of the old love has been created. This holds true for you too, the one reading this now. For there is a love that endures beyond distance, change, and radical shifts in energy and circumstances. There are those who are faithful, and to whom you have given your bond too. There is a love and faithfulness that endures, even beyond lifetimes. This is yours. Observe this miracle of everlasting trust and love. Be grateful. And give thanks.

BLESSING: Love is a miraculous state, and some loves are so powerful that destinies change, and lives are remade within the crucible of its fires.

CURSE: A belief that love is powerless when it comes to difficulties, or that it fades, its light dims.

WORKING WITH THIS CARD: Love can be renewed, reignited and enduring. Open your heart to the power of love. Know that it is a powerful force, and give it a place of honour in your life, your home, your work. Love is all there is. Work and live from that place where love dwells within you, and your life will be sublime.

25. *The Monster Within*

INTERNAL STRUGGLE, PERSONAL CHALLENGES, WANTING TO IMPROVE

LES VAMPIRES SPEAK: There is something we know more about than anyone could ever imagine. We are afraid never of the world, but of our ability to destroy something tender and beautiful within an instant, because our very nature ensures we hunger for something that will kill those we love if we take it. This is a terrible dilemma, for we are loveable, and loving – we know how to draw close, and how to be well, and in control, for many years. But at some time, in a moment of weakness, when defences are down and we hunger and our humanity is far away, we may snap, and our hunger may overrun the incredible control and balance we've had. We would never hurt you. And yet, our urge to love you is tied up with our urge to have you. We must learn vast powers of discipline. And this is what can lead us to vanish from the lives of those we care most for. If you are receiving this card, it would seem you too are struggling with an aspect of yourself that you know can bring harm to another, but which is a natural part of you – you are wrestling the demons that lie within.

BLESSING: Knowing our own faults and flaws can give us the tools to transform them into strengths.

CURSE: Unable to find the good in your own mistakes. Blind to the potential for change. Defining yourself only in negative terms.

WORKING WITH THIS CARD: If you begin to practice discipline each day, and create new ways of dealing with frustrations and difficulties, you will find your so-called negative traits can be reshaped, and who you are will be redefined. Changing yourself is a great purpose. This is yours at this time.

26. Jealousy

ENVY, PUNISHMENT, CHANGING COURSE

LES VAMPIRES SPEAK: The Lamia is a legendary creature, one of we Vampires, from the ancient lands of Greece. She was once the Queen of a land you now call Libya, her beauty so famed it drew the attention of the God Zeus, who gave her his love, and many children. For the crime of being so loved, she was cursed by the Goddess Hera, the long-suffering wife of Zeus. Lamia suffered Hera's spite, and was cursed to become a serpent from below the waist, and to hunger for the blood of her own children.

Overcoming spite and envy for your good fortune is the message Lamia has for you. Your desire to care for your own, your blessings and what you love has attracted envy from others. This has sparked guilt and fear within you. And now you are in danger of punishing yourself simply because another wishes you to be hurt. Instead of suffering, you can change. And you can become strong, even when there are those who wish to harm you, and who are powerful, as Hera is. Learn from Lamia's serpent self – the serpent is the Divine Feminine, and a being who sheds skin, mothers fiercely and who can feel the faintest of changes in energy and vibration. You too can sense the slightest change at the moment. You are able to anticipate any threats and any danger. She is unable to close her eyes – so her gift to you is to have your eyes wide open, to observe all the changes and to be honest about what you are undergoing. She is a strong card for you to have chosen – and if she has come to you, you have the ability to stay fierce, protect what you love, and connect with the Divine Feminine. It may also be that there is gossip about your appearance, and your sexual behaviour. Call those who speak against you out, name them, and declare yourself free. Do not allow anyone to question your behaviour when it is their own actions they are choosing to overlook.

BLESSINGS: The Lamia teaches us that you need not accept what people say about you. You are beyond their judgment. Their words are false. You need never live up to them. You are trustworthy, and a beautiful soul.

CURSE: There can be cruelty, bullying and difficulty in life. There is some of this about you at present. Words can be harmful – take steps to minimise the impact.

WORKING WITH THIS CARD: When you find yourself called "evil" or a "demon" or accused of doing harmful things, first examine your conscience. Now, all of us have made errors – most especially we Vampires. But the Lamia teaches you that you need not go mad with grief, or allow another's cruelty to curse you. You can rise above this, and be true to yourself. Live through example. Be strong. This time will pass. Remind yourself and others that those who speak ill, speak ill of all in their turn. None shall escape their turn.

27. *Ecstasy*

YIELDING, RAPTURE, BLISS

LES VAMPIRES SPEAK: The connection so many have with others who are vampiric in nature is that the giving up of will, and of force, and of being submissive towards another is a way of experiencing a kind of ecstasy. It is not a lack of power that enables you to experience this – to become soft and yielding, and to allow the will of another who is worthy to dominate is an experience of surrender. It is not helpless, or about giving up—it is a choice, for a time, to allow your own will to be dominated by the will of another—and in this experience, ecstasy can be found. For humans tire so often of having to be assertive – of again and again saying what they need, what they deserve, of working hard to not be hurt or eaten alive by a system or by jobs that do truly eat the souls of the people in them. If you could see what we see, the beautiful force fields around you of energy lessening and diminishing as you give, and give, and force yourself to be strong so often, until energy and self and body are worn and tired. There is restoration in the ecstasy of allowing a worthy other to advise, protect, guide and hold you for a time. It is ecstatic because for just that moment, we need not be concerned about our survival and the survival of all around us. The stress drops away and a deep, beautiful intoxicating surrender flows through you, just as it does when you submit to sleep, to deep relaxation, to the ministrations of another who, in that instance of that time, knows what will please you. Some believe this is all about the sexual dimension, but it is not – it can be about any part of life where you have fought, tried and struggled, and gathered your energy and surged through obstacles. Now it is time for the deep relaxation and restoration … to allow one about you, who is worthy, to give to you in ways that create an ecstatic experience, and a deep bond of trust. When we take a lover, when we fall in love, so deeply and passionately as we do, the ecstatic response of our beloved to our kiss, touch, words, is our greatest gift and our greatest pleasure. This we wish you to experience. But only with one worthy of your beautiful surrender.

BLESSING: The ability to surrender to a Higher Power, of your choosing, is a valuable experience, as well as one which can provide intoxicating levels of delight.

CURSE: Being enraptured is close to losing yourself – which is one of the keys to the ecstasy it creates. Be sure to stay in touch with your own soul, and have a close friend who can remind you of who you are.

WORKING WITH THIS CARD: There is power in the surrender, and great soul ecstasy in the finding of one who, for an instant, takes the burden of decisions and gives you great relief and satisfaction and pleasure. Be aware that you must choose this person with great care. It is time though, for you to admit that in some ways, ecstatic experiences are our teacher, only when chosen wisely.

28. *Burnt by the Sun*

AMBITION, EXTENSION, REACH

LES VAMPIRES SPEAK: There are times when you have set yourself a great task – when you have decided that you have within sights a glorious outcome. It could be an ambition, or a relationship, or a position, or an achievement. But the meaning of this card is a warning – a caution to you. There is much that can come to you simply and with ease – but there are things in this world, which we both share, that must be earned. You must earn this next step. For it is as it is for us. Our nature is to live in the night, to be under the gentle, brilliant light of the stars, of candles, of the last moments of sunset, or the first moments of sunrise. To be in the full glare of the light is not for us. And at this time—this time not for all time—the fullness of your ambition will not be available to you. It must be earned. It must be deserved. And there is a path to walk, and a road to take before you can get there.

You may of course decide that we do not know of what we speak, or of you, and your desire – and you may decide to reach as high as you can. And we say to you, when this sun you reach for burns you with its fire—for it is a star and made of fire—you will learn then what it is to be too eager, too soon. There is a time, and a place, and a way in which we earn what will be ours. The desire is worthy of you. You are worthy of reaching it. But for now, the dream, which you reach for, you are not yet ready for. There is more work for you to do first. Be wise.

BLESSING: You will never know your potential, unless you go beyond the limits you have set yourself. You may not succeed. But you will know a great deal more about yourself than you do now – and you are certain to grow through the experience. Begin with baby steps, and persist.

CURSE: Turning away from potential failure means you also turn away from potential success and growth. You avoid harm – but at a great cost. Or over-reaching without gaining experience.

WORKING WITH THIS CARD: You must be mindful of what is safe and wise for you at this time, with the skills and training you have. You have a way to go before your changes are made. It is as if you are wishing to undertake a marathon, without ever having run a mile. It is time to train, learn and become strong. In time, the desire will be within reach. Patience and hard work both are priorities for now. Otherwise there could be self-administered hurt and injury.

29. *Witness*

TO KNOW, PERSONAL EVIDENCE, TO SPEAK OUT

LES VAMPIRES SPEAK: To have seen what you once thought was only a rumour, or only hearsay, or perhaps even made up, means you have changed. And you have seen us. You have seen spirits. You have seen the play of colours around a human being, their auric field telegraphing information to you at all times. You have experienced the dream that comes true in the weeks after you saw faces in the night, you have spoken with the nature spirits and you have come to know there is more than what so many humans wish to admit is true and alive in the world we all share. Vampires like us, we are said not to exist. But you know there is more here on this planet than anyone can even begin to dream of. You know we are true. And you have witnessed something of late that others still deny is "real." But you are now a witness and having seen, you cannot un-see. Knowing, you can no longer deny. It is not that we wish for you to tell all of your new knowledge. It is that we wish you to not lie to yourself, to no longer agonise over questions of whether what you saw and felt and understood is true or untrue. There is so much on this planet of ours. Think of it. And you and I, though so different, are between us only two types of the millions of variations on the extraordinary creatures there are. Who is either of us to deny the truth of the wonder that is this planet and all the manifestations of life upon it? You have seen what some say is untrue. Know that it is not a lie. It would be a lie and harmful to you to deny what you know after the gift of this knowledge.

BLESSING: The veils of illusion and deceit have lifted. While this can be painful, it is also a great blessing to know the truth. Do not doubt your experience.

CURSE: It can be tempting to protest against being lied to, or hurt. Know that the road you are on will take you to many places, and this stop on the journey was necessary for you to take the next steps, wiser. You are now free. There is no curse with this card at all.

WORKING WITH THIS CARD: Know that what you have seen and felt is true. Another may deny that you have witnessed a true thing. But having seen and now knowing, you have a duty to never again lie to yourself. You need not make this truth your entire life. But never again lie to yourself. Accept the evidence of your experience, and honour it within your heart, and within your words when wisdom demands you speak freely. There are some who would betray your confidence. Others will share your experience, and become your kin when you share wisely.

30. *That Death Will Come*

MORTAL, FINITE, FRAGILE

LES VAMPIRES SPEAK: One day, as all of us must, you will die. What do these words strike into you? Fear? Resolution to live? Acceptance? Or is there simply a sense of what is not known. We have lived longer than humans, yet we are not so old as the cycle of life. We too will come to our ending, and we, just as you, do not know for certain what will take place. Will there be a void, an emptiness? A nothingness? Will there be peace? Will there be punishment? But one thing we can be sure of. There will be an ending. Those who tell you they know for sure what lies on the other side, believe them not. Because when we live, that is what we know. The flow and pulse of hot blood. We have the opportunity to be good – and when we say good, we mean fine, of quality. There may be nobility. When there is an ending of the kind that death is, we separate from those on the other side. There are those who speak with the dead, and listen to the spirits. That is good and well. But do not dwell on that. And do not deny that you will die. There are those who will try to sell you ways to lengthen your life. Give you prayers and spells to never die. But we tell you now, accept this you must. Even we die, and we live longer than even the fae.

Your mortality is beautiful. Of it is born compassion. The desire to live well and deeply. In the brevity of human spans is the impetus that drives you to explore, to go further, and to create rich experience. In the full understanding of your mortality and its beauty, you will begin to explore the potential of being alive, now. It matters not if you have many more lives to live, have lived before, or will live again. All that matters is now, and what you do with every moment you are blessed with.

BLESSING: Knowing that we have one lifetime at a time to make changes, learn lessons and move closer to the true purpose of our soul is a blessing. Knowing that each lifetime must not be wasted, and is precious, is a gift that compels us to lead lives of meaning.

CURSE: Knowing that our lives will end can lead to doubt and to fear. Even this can be turned to good purpose.

WORKING WITH THIS CARD: It is time to honestly create meaning in each day, and to choose to make the very best of the time you have. Every day is a gift. Make it count. It is time to live more fully, and to make a list of what your dreams and plans are. It is time to know that in whatever way you feel trapped, you are killing yourself before life is taken from you. Kill the thing that is killing you.

31. *Prey*

STALKED, INVADED, WATCHED

LES VAMPIRES SPEAK: When one is hunted in your time, with your people, you are often unable to identify what is happening. The veneer of civility that covers us all, even us, especially us, helps us appear kinder than we are. Some people are hunters. And that makes others prey. In your culture at this time, there is a theory that those who are harmed, or hurt have somehow attracted that to themselves. Oh, how the hunters love this argument. For it is a way of saying that the prey is offering itself up. And this is what we have come to warn you of. We have come to tell you that there is one who sees you as prey, and they see themselves as the hunter. And the more they can persuade you that you wish to play this role, and that it is your fault, the more powerful they will become. This card comes forth when one has been groomed to be hurt. There are many examples of abuse and monstrosity in your world, amongst humans. And often it is the one who is most close to you, who will take what is most precious to you. Do not become prey. And do not agree to this hunter being invited by you. The victimisation they are visiting upon you has not been invited by you, except through circumstance. There is no contract that means this must play out. If you feel this is wrong, speak up, and speak out. Being hunted, being preyed upon, is not something you must take the responsibility for, nor must this play out. You can change the script in the hunter's head. You can change the outcome. You can refuse to become prey. You can play this game quite differently to the script they have handed you. In fact, you need not play the part at all.

BLESSING: You are able to make a stand, and you are strong, clever and powerful.

It is time to stand up to a bully or to one who wishes to blame you for their own bad behaviour. You did not attract the circumstances you find yourself within. You have a great deal more power than they wish you to have.

CURSE: There are lies and manipulations taking place to make you accept the circumstance. You can change this, and say, clearly no – this is not right, and it is not for me.

WORKING WITH THIS CARD: Do not allow yourself to be prey for another's hunger. Do not refuse to help yourself, or fall into patterns of victimhood. Take good advice, demand what is yours by rights—including innocence— and be strong in the face of the one who would devour you. You cannot always win, but the greatest battle you face at present is the one within you that says "I give up. Nothing ever goes my way." It can, and it will, when you believe you are worth fighting for.

32. *Hunter*

AGGRESSOR, TRACKER, PROVIDER

LES VAMPIRES SPEAK: There is a belief that in order to have what it is we feel we need, or want, or desire, or are told we must have, we must track it, hunt it, and sometimes, kill it. For the hunter does not simply follow and make a friend of the creature it wishes to have. It must kill it, in order to be satisfied. There is a part of you that feels this falsehood – that in order to become something, there must be a death, of which you will be the cause. That there is competition, and need, and that you can only have what you long for if someone else can no longer have it. And we have come to you to say that even we, who are the unnatural world's greatest hunters, need not kill. There is always a way to find what we need, without taking it from another. There is within you now, an urge to win in a competition, where you feel there may only be one survivor. But there are other ways through to the goal you desire. You can find what it is you need deep within. And there is also truth in the word 'hunter'. For you to live each day, something must die. Be it for the food on your table, or the produce that has become your walls and the home you live in, energy has given up one form and become another. Everything transforms. But for that which you seek now, the hunt needs to go within. The chase must be of that part of your character which, when hunted down and integrated, will give you what you lack in order to create what you need. You need to become the hunter of the hidden parts of your own self, of the courage you feel you lack, of the opportunity you believe you have not been given. For you breathe, do you not? And as you breathe, you, a part of you, is the hunter, and must take action to obtain what it is you long for. No one else will do this for you. This task is yours alone, human.

BLESSING: It is natural and wise to allow the part of you that is active, and strong, and forceful, to have expression. It is time to actively seek that which you want. See how far your strength can take you.

CURSE: There is always the potential that the hunter can become ruthless. You can maintain discipline by focusing on what it is you seek, and refuse to be distracted by the pursuit of power for power's sake.

WORKING WITH THIS CARD: It is time to establish how to obtain what it is you want. You must not ask another to go after it. And while the hunt will take place on the outside, it will also take place on the inside. You must find that part of you within that has the courage to chase what you would make yours. And be honest about it.

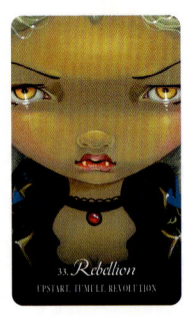

33. *Rebellion*

UPSTART, TUMULT, REVOLUTION

LES VAMPIRES SPEAK: There is about you an established order. There is about you a power that says things must be done in a particular way. That the order is rightful, and must be maintained. The freedom to question is being refused, and is considered to be offensive. The right to speak up, even respectfully, is being restrained. Those who find a new way to approach the old problems are considered dangerous. And for a time, now, you have kept silent. But there is a different way—many different ways—of approaching the same questions. Instead of each person having the right to approach the questions in a way that is true to them, you are being asked not to think, not to feel, but simply to follow. And you are tired of following when this following is taking you no closer to the adventures and solutions you wish to discover. But it is hard to be the one who speaks up. It is challenging to be the one to say there may be another way. For to do so in your place right now is to become a rebel. This sounds romantic, but it is not. It is a hard path to walk, yet it is the one you are being asked to set off on. And in doing so, you may find others wish to make you a new leader, and a new keeper of laws and orders. But for you, this is a personal journey, and you do not wish to influence any other to do anything but to know that following their own path, and finding their own way, may be best for them. It is a choice.

What lies before you is the fork in the road, which you will take not to be defiant, or to create dissonance … you follow it because it is the path of your heart. And you will be called rebel, you will be called difficult, and you will be told you are wilful, even egotistic. But you are not. You need not do this with fanfare and great noise. You simply take the turn that others do not, and you begin to walk alone. It is lonely. But the false camaraderie of conformity you leave behind frees you, and offers you true moments of joy, rather than false comforts.

BLESSING: You are being called to follow your own soul's path. It is a wonderful thing when you truly become yourself – and find what you love.

CURSE: There will be loneliness from time to time – but you will meet like-minded rebels upon your soul's road.

WORKING WITH THIS CARD: It is time to be truthful about who you are, and what it is you wish to create in your life. You can do this – there will be more support than you can dream of when you open up and share what you felt you must keep secret. There are more like you than you know.

34. *Discipline*

TRAINING, CONSISTENCY, PRACTICE

LES VAMPIRES SPEAK: You want something to be easier than it must be in order for you to value it. You want something to happen faster than it can for your own growth and stability. You are, in short, much like most humans we see. You lack discipline. There are times when we feel that in order to achieve something, or to reach a goal, we need only meditate upon it, visualise it as being real, and it will therefore come to us through the process you have come to call The Law of Attraction. There is another law. The law of contribution and hard work and tenacity. It has no pretty name. It offers no quick fix. But it is real and its results are lasting and true. And this is the lesson with you at present. There need be no stress, resentment or devaluation of what you will achieve simply because it did not arrive through effortless circumstance. The goal you have in mind is yours when you steel yourself to the hard work ahead. It will not be work that is wanted. It will require doing things that many feel are unpleasant. But that is only because you modern humans are being trained out of your abilities to take on great tests. There is a desire within your culture to at all times experience happiness and comfort. It has created generations of people who are physically unwell, mentally lazy, and spiritually apathetic. The discipline that is being required of you will result in a great breakthrough. You know that a major part of your life requires a change, and the brutal truth, which we give you here, is that this will be hard. You must not wait for motivation and desire. You must commit, and build the discipline to carry through this plan that will see so many blessings able to enter your life. Carving out the doorway will take willpower, action, and showing up, again and again.

BLESSING: You have the ability to create a program of change, and stick to it, and after a period of time, it will transform from painful to pleasurable. The freedom and strength it affords you far outweigh the pain you experience in the short term.

CURSE: Self-doubt could compromise the potential you now have. Do not allow this! This challenge you face will go beyond what is easy and pleasant to do, and yet it will bring you all that you wish for, and the strength of character you sometimes have doubted you have.

WORKING WITH THIS CARD: It is time to lay a plan down, to create structure, and to stick to commitments. You must clear doubt, and into the space its absence creates, pour action.

35. *Sacrifice*

RENUNCIATION, OFFERING, LETTING GO

⤝────────────────────⤞

LES VAMPIRES SPEAK: In humans' lives, there is a great resistance to choice. And you may ask of us, what is choice to do with sacrifice, the name upon this card? But choice is at the very heart of sacrifice. For life, with its multiplicities of possibilities, demands that you make your choices. And for many of you, we notice again and again that you refuse to make the choice. And then, you are forced to make one, but one that suits another. It is time for you to examine what you value most, and what you would least wish to give up. The word 'sacrifice', and we know this as we have lived long, is a way of making the thing you give up sacred. It is a loss. It is painful. It matters. Therefore the void that is left means something, and must be filled with something that means more. For so many of you, you will not choose. You wish to be good to all. You wish to let down none. You do not think about what is best. For what is best is that which sets your blood alight, and makes the song of your soul soar. What is best is that you know your own heart, and know your own code, and adhere as closely as possible to what is noble about you. There will not be time for all, space for all, love for all. You may protest – you may wonder, what of loving everyone unconditionally? But that is an illusion. Even in love, you must choose.

So, we say now, you must sacrifice something. You must give up something that is precious. By doing so, make it beautiful. Make it worth it. Make it count. And make this deliberate. Do not play victim. Make your choice, and be powerful and compassionate at once.

BLESSING: Your compassion, heart and empathy will grow as a result of the sacrifice you now are being asked to make. Not by another. But by your own soul. You are strong enough to do this. But you have never known for sure, because you have never put yourself to the test. Now you will. And you will see just how strong you truly are.

CURSE: You doubt you can give this up. Perhaps you feel you are weak. Excuses have been your refuge before this time. But now, you are ready.

WORKING WITH THIS CARD: There is something you may need to give up – it could be that in order to do what you know to be right for your soul, you must let go of something that in many ways gratifies, excites and soothes you. It could be the sacrifice of sleep in the morning to get up and run. It could be the sacrifice of the luxury of a pay cheque, in order to explore your true calling. It could be the letting go of comfort, in order to explore. It could be the sacrifice of your personal time, in order to devote yourself to one who needs your care at this time. Whatever it is, choose. And then, know this sacrifice can be worked with and used to refine and polish your character – so that you become more the offspring of angels than you already are.

36. *Faith*

TRUST, UNWAVERING, CONFIDENCE

LES VAMPIRES SPEAK: The belief that something will take place, or is right, or is a particular way, can be called faith. Faith is quiet and hopeful, offers contentment and calm, it has not bravado, and it need not insist on its rightness. Faith is something we have too, and we observe it in the best of those we call humans, the warm-blooded ones of whom you are one. It is a beautiful gift that you humans have to be believers in this quiet, gentle way. Faith is not always beautifully expressed. Faith is a loving, amazing quality, but it must be attached to something that is worthwhile. When this card arrives at your door, it is best to examine what it is you have faith in. What is faith to you? Were you taught faith as a child, and did you lose faith at one point? For you are often taught to believe in things that do not deserve your faith. It may now be time to relearn what it is you have enduring constant hope for – what you know will come to be, even if your eyes may never see it. And we know about Faith … the persistent notion that all will be well in time. For we live with this faith. Without it, we would be dead inside.

The human spirit has faithfulness at its core, at its best. To have faith is to remain loyal, but in a truly heartfelt way.

Tender, moving and full of grace, your faith may soon return to you. Choose wisely in what you place this gift of your faith.

BLESSING: Your faith returns, and you feel a true connection and comfort in your choices and plans. They are supported by the energy of the universe.

CURSE: Feeling jaded and hurt by what you have learned, you have lost some of your enthusiasm and innocence.

WORKING WITH THIS CARD: If you have lost faith in a person, project, or humanity itself, it is time to examine the source of the faith. Know that it can be revived, and this time, you may choose where you place this most beautiful and tender of faiths.

37. *Religion*

CANON, RULES, COMMANDMENTS

LES VAMPIRES SPEAK: Religion has been through so much with you humans. We have watched it change, moment to moment it would seem. Every thousand years or so your Gods have changed, your faiths have changed, and people everywhere have died, again and again, for the rightness of all you say is right and true. We watch, and wonder, for we too have this within us – the world in which we lived as humans has stamped us, marked us, and even now, we find ourselves moved at the sight of the Cross, or drawn to a cathedral where countless pilgrims have worshipped. Yet we wonder at this thing … this thing called religion. For you have made vows not only in this life – as one of the many-born, you are unlike us. You can recall the lives of long ago, and at times, there are vows and structures you have carried with you from life to life, the tattered remnants of belief and the sharp knives of punishment follow you, lifetime after lifetime, and all the while you say, I am not religious. I am spiritual. But you are religious. There is much about you that is nun, monk, apostle, pilgrim, abbot, priest, shaman. You are and have been so much, so many things, and religion has been drunk in at your mother's breast and formed so much of who you are. Become aware, we say, of this. No longer deny this, we ask. For you, unlike us, will be born again and again, and when you understand what it is this framework of understanding the world has given to you—and what it has also stolen from you—you will come to a place where your own soul has room to breathe. For religion, and religious beliefs may have given humanity purpose and survival strategies – but it has simultaneously suffocated the true expressions of their souls. It is a vast form of black magick. And we have all dabbled in it. It is time to wash it clean – but first, we must know what it is we have, what no longer helps us, and what we choose to believe and become, from this day forth.

BLESSING: The structure and family feeling of revealed religions can feel safe and secure for many. They can also harness great energies, which can be directed for good. There is also great beauty in the rites and rituals, history and tradition.

CURSE: The need to adhere to strict beliefs means most souls will give their power away – and their connection to the Divine. Power concentrates in the hands of the few – and can be abused.

WORKING WITH THIS CARD: Learn more of the world's religions, and begin to understand what has influenced your own life, and your own culture, even your laws and the conditions under which you live. While this may sound exhausting, it will be helpful, as you begin to understand a difference between personal ethics, faith and connection …

and a religion that was revealed to another, and which you have been ordered, even indirectly, to make your own. Now it is time to examine your heart. And say, this is mine. This is what I worship. This is what I love.

38. *Courtesy*

THOUGHTFUL, POLITE, GOOD MANNERS

LES VAMPIRES SPEAK: One thing we are known for, in the main, is our exquisite manners. Although this little Vampire has no need for food, she has made sure her guests are going to be provided for with the sweetest of treats at her moonlit feast. So know that we think of your needs. Manners, we do have. Manners are not simply a façade to veil our cruelty, or the terrible hunger that creates that cruelty. Manners are a way of gracefully doing what must be done, to smooth the difficulties we all must face, and to create beauty amongst days that can be full of crude squalor. Having manners is to think of others' comfort, and what will please them. This card we bring to you this day speaks to you of the need under the current circumstances to speak the truth, but to do so with grace and diplomacy and the least offence possible. This means to work out what it is you wish to achieve in the forthcoming discussions, and how to best appease the offence, which has already flared. With manners, diplomacy and thoughtfulness, you may still navigate this treacherous stretch of your life. It is worth being kind, truthful, and yet graceful. In many of the nations in which we have travelled, we have noticed that in those which have manners, gracefulness and dignity, there is a great deal of honour and there is often harmony amongst people living in even the most difficult and testing of circumstances. Manners are not insincere within themselves, although they can be, when used to mask hostility. But the crime there is hypocrisy. The time has come to marry up grace, with truth, and consideration. Use the beautiful, magickal gift of your good sense, and your charm, and watch doors open, and problems dissolve with newfound understanding.

BLESSING: Thinking of others creates flow, and the energy shall return to you, to the power of three by three. Beauty and grace create harmony in social interactions.

CURSE: Thoughtless actions can impede the flow of energy, waste time, and create negative potential.

WORKING WITH THIS CARD: It may seem strange – a Vampire speaking of manners, when they so often have been known to take life. But they have often not done so, and they have also made friends and allies amongst those who were once most opposed to them. This is because they are charming, their manners are often delightful, and they are able to speak with heart and truth, but to see the beauty within all, and the need, and address that. Learn manners for the new places you are going, and be courteous as well as truthful.

39. *Supernatural*

INEXPLICABLE, MIRACULOUS, OTHERWORLDLY

LES VAMPIRES SPEAK: There are many things in the world that most people cannot explain away conveniently. That includes Vampires. Like this beautiful silver haired creature surrounded by flying fish as the sun breathes its last behind her. Before her is a surreal vision. And yet, there it is. Real, yet unreal at the same time. And we are scientists and we are doctors and we teach and we walk amongst you. And we hear so many times of what is said to be impossible: the hearing of thoughts. The moving of objects through energy. The knowing of events before they occur. The receiving of messages from Spirit realms. The ability to see colours around bodies. The ability to heal through touch. And I tell you all that these are not 'supernatural'. They are natural. And when they are developed and worked upon, and exercised and practiced with, they are considered super. You have these qualities. You have them in abundance. And we can see them about you. It is your task now to develop them. Not to develop them without reason and intelligence – but to develop them and to celebrate your nature, your magnificent humanity which has such potential, and which is so vital to all of us. You are supernatural. You are as magnificent as those who are in spirit. You are a divine creation. And it is now time for you to celebrate this, to embrace this, and to become as strong in your extra senses as you are in others. Embrace yourself, human child. All of your magickal, wondrous self.

BLESSING: There are aspects to you that are divine, and utterly connected to all the cycles and aspects of nature. You now feel secure and safe in developing and expressing your intuitive gifts more than ever before.

CURSE: Feeling fearful and nervous about using your intuitive gifts. Beliefs that such powers are dangerous, or negative. Feeling unworthy, or unsafe.

WORKING WITH THIS CARD: It is time now to begin to understand that the senses we all have are not special gifts given only to the chosen. We all have them. You may have been despairing at your own lack of gifts, and wondering what your own abilities may be. It is time to discover this by paying attention, and through hard work.

40. *Natural*

AUTHENTIC, REAL, ORGANIC

LES VAMPIRES SPEAK: To be your own true self is a lifelong—lifetimes long—purpose. It is the purpose of this existence, and for each of us, despite the labels we all have – human, vampire, woman, man. We have something greater at play – how the essence, that very drop of pure self makes itself known through us. And for this great miracle to take place, there are habits to be shed, reactions to be questioned, challenges to be met, and experiments to be made. For you are not who you have been told you are. And so with this card, we ask for you to clearly and finally, perhaps understand and acknowledge that all that you are can be discovered when you take yourself within, and quietly feel, look and listen to your own self. Not the self of the label, the job. Not the defences you have developed for protection. Not the protests of ego, or the demands of family voices within. It is who you truly are. And then, once having found a sense of that, to live from that place in small, consistent ways each day. How that manifests will be unique for each of you. But we ask for you now to go beyond the labels of time, and place, and family, and education, and status – and go deep, deep within. There is something within you that is more than the history of others. That is yours alone. And the world needs it to be expressed – otherwise, why would you have been created? For each of us – every drop of rain, every stone, every creature of the sky and the land, has their role and their part to play. We need to become our natural self again, beyond what we are told we are, and to live from that place. And this will create a satisfying and more peaceful, harmonious life – no matter what challenges you meet from within, or without. You are precious to the world, especially so when you find that part of you that is only yours to offer, and add it to the song of the world, and make all that is more beautiful, more fulfilled, and more totally realised as a consequence of your soul's truest expression.

BLESSING: When you take away the trappings of money, power, status in the world, you are left with the things of the spirit. And you are rich in the ways of the soul indeed. This creates a balanced, centred strong core.

CURSE: Too much reliance on the feedback of society. Self-worth is centred in status, and therefore is constantly shifting. Uncentred.

WORKING WITH THIS CARD: There has been an over-reliance on ways of identifying who you are – whether you have categorised yourself by a job, or your appearance, personality or wealth and background, it is time to go beyond this, to who you truly are, and know yourself from the inside out. This does not require puzzlement and complexity. It requires quiet, distilment, and true reflection and contemplation of the self. You have too many definitions others have given you. Let them go. And learn the song within you, and give voice to that, in order to become natural, and truly fulfilled as your own self.

41. *Transgression*

FLAWS, CONTRADICTIONS, MISTAKE

LES VAMPIRES SPEAK: There are many in this world, Vampire and human, faery and otherworldly creature, who seem to delight in the faults of others, using them as a way of proving their own worth. See, they point out. You are worse than I! And could there be any worse than this killing of a sacred animal, the Unicorn, now mourned so deeply by this little Vampire. This is false glory, and disturbing to all of us who live long lives, to see so many worry that they have sinned and hurt others and cannot be forgiven, and to see others glory in the guilt they use to manipulate and feel righteous. The most perfected souls upon this planet have all created moments in their lives where they have gone against their own values, and their own hearts, their own souls … and transgressed. They have hurt themselves, as they have hurt others. And so, when you see this card, and wonder what it is you have done wrong, know it is this. It is incorrect of you to assume that your faults and flaws, your poor decisions, and yes, the mistakes you have made are more ghastly than any other. There is not one amongst any of us who has not done wrong. And it is good that we Vampires and you humans can feel remorse, and take steps to correct ourselves, and do better. But what we witness from here is that you are being told, again and again, by either an abusive other, or your own abusive part of yourself, that you are guilty, wrong, and can never be forgiven. You must now take steps to correct what can be corrected, apologise clearly and once if this is the right thing for you to do, and then forgive your own self. To continually internally erode your own value due to another's encouragement is a false kind of virtue. There is no good in hurting yourself, over and over, to prove how sorry you are. Live better, do better, but let the self-punishment go, and do not allow another to utilise your compassionate remorse for their own ends. Yes, they are. We are all—human, and otherworld creature —going to transgress against the natural laws and the laws of our own souls. What we do about it is what matters. Go on now and make amends, then give thanks for the gift of self-forgiveness.

BLESSING: When we go against our integrity, our soul will let us know. And if we continue to deny that inner voice, the universe will show us where we are going wrong.

CURSE: Crowding out our inner voice, continuing down a path that we know is against the truth of our soul, breaking universal laws.

WORKING WITH THIS CARD: Make amends. Take stock, assess, and redirect, and come back into harmony with the voice of your soul.

42. *Nobility*

HONOUR, HIGH STANDARDS, IDEALISTIC

LES VAMPIRES SPEAK: There is something within you that we, the Vampires, can recognise at this moment. We want you now to focus on it, recognise it and acknowledge it. You have nobility. People—humans, that is—are so often confused by this word, feeling one must be from an old and aristocratic family to have any noble blood within them. But some of the most corrupt; indecent and coarse humans and Vampires have had aristocratic origins. You have shown nobility of spirit, and action, and you have behaved in a manner which has drawn our attention. We wish to encourage you to behave in these noble ways more often. Nobility is a sense of innate virtue, or being able to do what is best and right within circumstances that would have been easier had we simply fallen into step with the prevailing thinking. You have helped the helpless. You have protected one who was weaker. You have spoken for the voiceless. You have been virtuous with no thought of reward. But this is the reward you did not ask for, but deserve. For you are as a Knight, or Lady, in the most chivalrous of tales, and you have lived with grace, and are becoming a more refined being with every day. Vampires, when we have learned to live beyond the instincts our new nature gives us, can be noble creatures too – and we must fiercely fight to become so. And so we, who have lived according to a code of nobility, wish to honour you now, and say, you have done well. Accept the acknowledgement. And know that the good deeds you have done so selflessly will ripple out into the world, and make changes you may never see, but your soul will know you made all the difference to one who was helpless, and to whom you gave your aid. We honour you, noble Sir, noble Lady.

BLESSING: This is a wonderful opportunity to do the very best you can, which in turn will shift your vibration, and attract wonderful new opportunities with honourable people to you.

CURSE: If you deny the nobility within you, it will become easy to go for the lowest option, again and again. This will sully your soul.

WORKING WITH THIS CARD: With this card's presence, you are asked to tune into that part of yourself that some of you call "The Higher Self." You are being asked to do the right thing, and do the best thing, even if it is not the most advantageous thing, or the easiest thing. You are also being asked, for a time, to be of service and assistance for others, and to give.

43. *Hope*

ANTICIPATION, BRIGHT PROSPECTS, WISH

LES VAMPIRES SPEAK: This little creature, this small one, a Vampire with a heart and soul, is surrounded by death. By endings. By sadness. By the void. And by those who have left her. Like you, she is facing the darkness within others and within life, and she feels utterly alone. But what she has with her is the ability to hope. And she chooses this. It is not something that is always easy, but she has lit a candle in the deep darkness, upon a heap of skulls and nothing else, and she has struck a light, and held up the light. She is quietly defiant in the face of death, of change, of silence, of loneliness, of criticism, and of a great dilemma. If this card finds you at this time, you are being asked to rise above those who are giving in to hopelessness and negativity. It does not ask you to be falsely hopeful, or to put on a happy face and refuse to face what must be faced. It asks you to be hopeful. You do not yet know the outcome. You do not yet know what will next happen. But what you can be assured of is that this hope that you have the capacity to create will sustain you in a time of great difficulty. Keep it strong, quiet, small even. Face what you must face. Do what must be done. And know that yes, this situation is very difficult. No doubt about it at all. But we Vampires ask you to know that one of the most beautiful and life-affirming things any of us can do is refuse to give in, and not only that, to do what must be done with hope. That light will attract help, intervention, assistance, and our admiration and respect, which in turn will deliver more assistance. You know there is some optimism you can create. You know you are the bearer of the torch, of the light, in this circumstance. And you know this hope will warm, inspire and nurture others. Lighten up the world you are within. Strike the light, and watch the shadows and dangers recede to the corners. Keep the flame burning.

BLESSING: Your ability to create possibilities in a seemingly hopeless and difficult situation brings out the best in others, which has a strong ripple effect. You have manifested change, through this hopefulness.

CURSE: Without hope, we lose heart. If hope feels futile for you, know that the act of hoping, of choosing to believe there are still reasons to look forward with optimism, will create a more positive outcome than you are looking at in the present moment.

WORKING WITH THIS CARD: You will soon have hope, which will make whatever is taking place at this moment easier to bear. This hardship is impermanent, and tomorrow will be better.

44. *Resurrection*

REPRISE, RECOVERY, COMEBACK

LES VAMPIRES SPEAK: Like the nine-lived Vampire kitties in this beautiful image, you too have more than one chance, more than one life. You have before you at this moment not just a second chance. You have a true new start in front of you. You have a chance to make over your life, and rise from what you thought was a stagnant place and have adventures. Recreation. We Vampires know only too well what it is like to arise from death – to transform from one kind of being, to quite another. The same, and yet so changed. You have almost given up on yourself. Almost lost touch with your enthusiasm for life. You have thought sometimes, maybe this is it, and found some kind of comfort in what you call acceptance. But we are here to show to you that in front of you, right at your feet, right in this moment, is the chance you have secretly dreamed of for so long. You have the chance to completely change your life. And if you choose to take up the offer of this card, of your life being remade and renewed, be assured that the very best of yourself, that never had the chance for expression before, will now have its moment. But it requires that you arise, shake off the past, and start again. You can be as one who was dead, who is now reborn. You have so much more to do, to give, to become – put away all thoughts that your life was static and decided upon. You have forgiven yourself. Now you must remake your own life.

This is a wonderful time to look for a new job, make important changes in your home with renovations, or move countries, change career, and even change your appearance – naturally, of course. Everything you need to revive and continue with renewed optimism and energy is with you at this time. The Vampires, the experts on new life, confirm that it is so. You are about to rise again. And those who will be surprised, will be inspired to change their own lives in the places that need it most.

BLESSING: This change can be made, and swiftly. Ask for assistance and it will be yours. Let go now, and move swiftly through the transition.

CURSE: You may feel that in order to change, you must pretend. We wish you to know that you have many facets to you: this new life will bring you astonishing new gifts, and it has come to you for a reason.

WORKING WITH THIS CARD: It is time to make things happen for yourself. It is time to actively explore what you have always denied yourself the chance to do. For there is a path clearing before you – but it requires an enormous amount of determination on your behalf. You must remake yourself. Look within and see what has less than satisfied you. And know that something that you thought was over, done with, and decided, is truly about to surprise you.

Lucy Cavendish is a true free spirit: a Witch and writer whose works are cherished and trusted around the world. An exciting voice in the field of inspiration, she is loved for her vision, compassion, wisdom and humour. She has that rare ability – to connect deeply with her readers.

Her work is notable for its breadth and depth of knowledge on sacred rites and sites, magickal history, witchcraft, folklore, alternative spiritual practices and intuitive traditions. Lucy's original creations have struck a chord with contemporary seekers ready to create lives of courage, spiritual adventure and magick.

Lucy's books and oracle decks are available in many languages, and she's a popular guest on television programs such as *Studio Ten*, *The Project* and *The Morning Show*. When she's not writing or recording her popular podcast, The Witchcast, you'll find Lucy drinking tea, surfing in the ocean or wandering deep within a faery forest.

You can discover more about Lucy by finding her on social media, listening to her podcast: *The Witchcast*.

ABOUT THE ARTIST

JASMINE BECKET-GRIFFITH is a traditional acrylic painter whose work blends realism with fantasy and the surreal. Historical and spiritual references are intertwined with fairytales and the beauty of nature. Her signature liquid-eyed maidens evoke deep emotions, drawing viewers into richly detailed narratives that transcend the ordinary. Her goal is to bring a bit of magic and mystery to the mundane world with every painting!

Jasmine's artwork is featured in many books and magazines, as well as countless merchandising lines such as the Bradford Exchange and Hamilton Collection, and her artwork with the Walt Disney Company, Lucasfilm, and more. Her paintings have a very wide appeal, appearing in public and private collections throughout the world, and she maintains an ever-growing legion of fans from all walks of life with her *Strangeling*™ brand.

A professional artist since 1997, Jasmine is a full-time painter based in Long Beach, California. Her work is showcased in galleries across the U.S., including the Corey Helford Gallery in Los Angeles, Disney's WonderGround Galleries, Art of Disney and Disney Galleries in Disney Springs.

strangeling.com

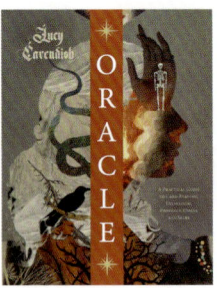

ORACLE OF THE SHAPESHIFTERS

Lucy Cavendish • Artwork by Jasmine Becket-Griffith

Messages and wisdom from magickal familiars, once the companions of shamans, witches, wizards, and wise ones, are now here for you. Trustworthy and wise, your newfound companions will lend you their courage, point out new paths, help you make fresh discoveries, and spark your creativity. Be inspired as they teach you to adapt and change, not only for survival but for thriving and finding peace, joy, accomplishment, and satisfaction in a changing world.

45 Cards & Guidebook • isbn: 978-0-9808719-3-7

ALICE: THE WONDERLAND ORACLE (Pocket Edition)

Lucy Cavendish • Artwork by Jasmine Becket-Griffith

Welcome to this whimsical, delightful pocket oracle, filled with the wit and wisdom of Wonderland. Inspired by Alice's most famous insights and adventures, you'll discover beings whose messages will help you find your way through the rabbit holes, labyrinths, pools of tears, mad tea parties and unjust courts of life. Prepare to meet the best-loved characters of Wonderland, all captured in stunning paintings by acclaimed artist Jasmine Becket-Griffith.

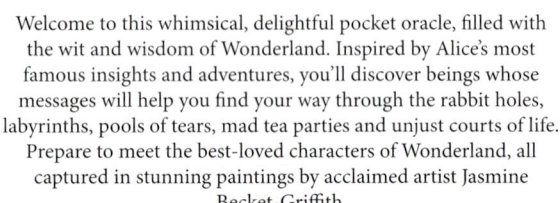

45 Cards & Guidebook • isbn: 978-1-922574-32-9

DRAGONLING COLORING BOOK

Jasmine Becket-Griffith

Jasmine Becket-Griffith is back – this time, with DRAGONS!

Jasmine has returned with 58 of her favorite dragonlings to delight and enchant adults and children alike. From the Emerald Guardian to the Valentine Dragon, the Halloween Dragon to the Dice Dragonlings, these drawings of Jasmine's beloved characters are perfect for those who want to lose themselves in the meditative details of her intricate yet simple style.

Each page encourages you to unleash your imagination and bring to life the magical potential of the dragons and fairies within. Grab your favorite coloring tools, settle in your happy place, and let your artistic spirit soar in the company of dragons!

128-PAGE BOOK • ISBN: 978-1-922574-43-5

NOTES

For more information on this
or any Blue Angel Publishing® release,
please visit our website at:

www.blueangelonline.com